# Conformed to His Likeness

# Conformed to His Likeness

{ BUILDING CHARACTER LIKE CHRIST }

LEROY LAWSON

Standard
PUBLISHING

CINCINNATI, OHIO

All Scripture quotations, unless otherwise indicated, are taken from
the HOLY BIBLE, NEW INTERNATIONAL VERSION®. NIV®.
Copyright © 1973, 1978, 1984 by International Bible Society. Used by
permission of Zondervan. All rights reserved.

ISBN 0-7847-7209-6

Edited by Lynn Perrigo
Cover design by Liz Malwitz

Standard Publishing, Cincinnati, Ohio
A division of Standex International Corporation
© 2004 by Standard Publishing
All rights reserved
Printed in the United States of America

# Contents

# INTRODUCTION

# Character—
# Can It Be Built?

"There is nothing wrong with having nothing to say—
unless you insist on saying it," said someone anonymously.
This bit of wisdom was never far from my mind while I wrestled with this book. Personal character is a huge theme. What
do I have to say about it that hasn't often been said and said
better than I can do it? Yet when Standard Publishing asked me
to prepare this Bible study book specifically on the character of
Christ, I couldn't resist. In writing I would be like the elderly
lady in E. M. Forster's *Aspects of the Novel* who was overheard
to say, "How do I know what I think until I see what I say?"
I wanted to know what I think and could hardly wait to see
what I would say.

I had no delusions about presenting a definitive study. The
human species is complex and intriguing, cleverly deflect-
ing the most learned efforts at defining it. What distinguishes
humans from animals? Among their many characteristics,
which are innate? Which do we have to strive for? Some men
and women rise above the others. What makes them better?

Why are we drawn to them and repelled by others? What do we mean when we compliment someone as a person of "real character"? I wanted to learn the answers to these questions.

Concentrating on Jesus would help me find them. On these pages He is presented as the ultimate man of character. Many regard Jesus more like an idol to be revered than as a model to be imitated. In this study, He is the latter. When He called His disciples, He intended more than that they should pick up certain skills for plying a trade; He was (and is) asking them (and us) to become like Him. "Follow my example, as I follow the example of Christ," the apostle Paul would later write to Christians in Corinth (1 Corinthians 11:1). No one else deserved such devotion. For all disciples, there is only one peerless model. We want to look like Him.

It takes more than wanting to though. We study His character precisely because He towers so far above us. The following chapters look closely at specific virtues that Jesus exemplifies. To master even one of them demands the best we have to give; to accomplish all 10 is almost beyond imagining. The goal of character building is not for the timid. It never has been. The truth is, we don't really know our own characters until they're tested. If you are . . .

> Honest until tempted,
>
> merciful unless it's uncomfortable for you,
>
> committed to a course until something more alluring comes along,
>
> or brave except when threatened,

you just think you have character. As C. S. Lewis pointed out, even Pilate was merciful until it became too risky for him.

So it is one thing to study the character of Jesus; it is quite another to "put on Christ"—that is, to adopt His character. To do so requires courage.

*Conformed to His Likeness* was designed for group study, but I hope you'll find it helpful for your personal reading and reflection as well. The book is just one disciple's meditation on what it takes to become more like the master.

A word about some of the illustrations is in order. They are personal, coming from my own experiences and reading. Many will perhaps surprise you because they come from secular sources—histories, biographies, politics, literature, business, and the arts. I long ago concluded that scriptural teachings are not holy words meant for holy places and events alone, but universal truths that are quite at home in a secular environment. In fact, if the teachings do not apply in "the world," they don't apply, period.

A small book like this can't do justice to the subject, so *Conformed to His Likeness* can't be more than a brief introduction. If it encourages you to do a further study of the Gospels in order to become better acquainted with Jesus' character—and with the person you wish to emulate—then it has accomplished its purpose.

# 1

# Built to "Come Down"

### Luke 2:1-20

{
And she gave birth to her firstborn, a son
. . . and placed him in a manger, because
there was no room for them in the inn
(Luke 2:7).
}

Which force is more responsible for the person you are—
heredity or nurture? Not very long ago experts were at each
other's throats over this question. Did your genes provide the
mold for you or did environmental pressures? Which is more
responsible—the physical determinants you received from your
parents (DNA) or what your parents did to you (discipline,
relationships, example, home environment) when you were in
their care? If you believe today's media, the debate is over. The
genes have it. The latest genetic discoveries are capturing the
headlines. Are you too fat? Blame your genes. Are you gay?
Undoubtedly genetic. Do you have trouble making friends?
The fault lies in your DNA. And there's noise that the genes for
alcoholism have been isolated, along with those for drug and
tobacco dependency.

Many of the studies are fairly persuasive. Pushed to their
extreme, however, they sometimes reduce human beings to
automatons: we behave as we are programmed to behave,

hardware obeying software. And our parents? Well, they just passed on the controlling genes at our conception. All their efforts to shape our personalities and form our characters were largely exercises in futility. When the genes speak, there's no talking back.

So it seems. Yet good parents continue to do their best to influence their children's behavior and help form the responsible adults they hope they will become. Parents have their vital role to play, as do schools and teachers, though they may not be nearly as influential as we once believed. Movies and television hold greater sway than educational institutions, it appears. If that's true, what can be said for Sunday schools? What are they good for? Can they really improve Johnny's behavior and Suzie's spiritual development? Are they, as even many nonreligious parents believe, beneficial for children's character formation?

The jury is still out. We are powerfully directed, probably even mostly directed, by our genetic inheritance. Study your own family. Traits keep turning up generation after generation. Not just physical characteristics either, but personality and character types wend their way. You heard about them in your great-great-grandparents, and now you are watching their latest incarnation in your grandchildren. But should we conclude that, unlike these physical bodies we have to accept (like them or not), we can do nothing about our personalities and are stuck with our flawed characters because they run in the family? I don't think so.

When we revisit the story of Jesus' birth in search of insight into His character, these questions won't go away. We want to know how He got to be who He was. He is called Son of Man and Son of God. What is the relationship of nature and nurture in this unique person? To what extent are we like Him? Or can we become like Him? In raising these questions, we join the centuries of thoughtful students before us. Theologians have argued and church councils have voted to settle the issue once and for all, but an issue of such magnitude can never be voted away. The words have changed over the years (our ancestors didn't know about DNA), but the questions remain basically the same.

The reason for launching this study of the character of Jesus is to help us become more like Him. But if we are nothing more than the product of genetic programming, and if Jesus was so much Son of God that He wasn't genuinely human (that is, His was superhuman DNA, nothing like ours), then this study is doomed before it starts.

Thus, I must show my hand at the outset. While admitting that so much of who we are is a given and that we have no control over it (do you think I would have *chosen* to be short?), we still have ample room to grow. We can change; we *do* change, whether we want to or not. Here, then, is the presupposition this book rests on: The characteristics we admire in Jesus are not out of reach for His disciples. We can put on the character of Christ if we want to.

## The Son of God Came Down

We begin at the beginning. According to Luke, the one we call Messiah, master, Lord, and Son of God and Man was born in the humblest possible circumstances. No room in the inn. Cradled in a manger, the sounds and smells of animal life penetrated the air. Angels in the heavens appeared to shepherds. It was no fit place, no fit company for the birth of divinity.

Jesus' story is not the only story of someone rising from the poorest of prospects to the pinnacle of power. (Abraham Lincoln comes immediately to mind.) Wise counselors to kings have long believed young princes should spend some of their formative years among common folk. They will be better monarchs if they know their subjects well. They may be of royal blood (nature), but their proper training (nurture) includes mingling with their future subjects.

So Jesus, who will rise the highest of all, was born to commoners, sheltered with the animals, forced with His parents to flee to Egypt like common refugees, and apprenticed to a carpenter's trade. For all His genetic wealth, He "came down" for further nurturing for the mission ahead.

I lead seminars for ministers and lay leaders. Here is another area of human development in which the jury is still out. Are leaders made or born? As nearly as I can tell, the answer is yes to both. They emerge from the womb with genetic leadership potential. (Yet even as I type these words, I am thinking of some glaring exceptions I know—men and women who have reached the pinnacles of their professions without the characteristics of "strong natural leaders.") However, most effective leaders have supplemented their DNA "givens" with study, experience, hard work, and often fanatical dedication to their goals.

If Luke's account of Jesus' birth and early childhood illustrates any leadership principle, it would be humility. But if I announced "humility" as a seminar topic, I could count on a drastic drop in attendance. Who has ever heard of humility as a requirement for leadership? You can't be serious! They might have heard of servant leadership, might even have been curious to know what it's about, but when they learn that it's about putting others first, taking the lowest seats, building others up even if it means not getting any credit themselves, well, they'll attend someone else's seminar, thank you.

At first I'd have a little trouble defending myself. The truth is, you can read a library of books on leadership without ever encountering *humility*. Leaders, the pundits will tell you, are usually dynamic, forceful, visionary, and charismatic men and women. They demand—and get—their way; they persuade—or browbeat—others to their point of view; they take charge; they win. They are sometimes proud, often overbearing, but never, ever humble.

Thus the stereotype. But here, as in so many other ways, Jesus shatters the stereotype. Do you know of a more successful leader in all of history? His work on earth was finished 2,000 years ago, yet the church He founded is the largest religious body on the globe today and still growing. Not bad for some-one "born in a barn."

So bear with me in this virtual leadership seminar as we explore what Jesus' "coming down" means for people who want to become more like Him.

## Come Down to Where the People Are

One of the mysteries of the Christian faith is why God, who could have arranged things any way He wanted, chose to have Jesus dwell among humanity, immersing himself in human experience and suffering temptation, rejection, loneliness, and heartache as well as enjoying joy, love, friendship, and laughter. An all-powerful God could have accomplished His purposes any way He wanted to.

What He wanted was for the Savior to come down to the people. To lead them, not to drive them. To inspire with hope and not dread. To serve and not to be served. To deliver grace rather than establish a meritocracy in which only the hardest workers, or the most deserving or talented, had any hope. The apostle Paul says in Philippians 2:6-8 that Jesus, "being in very nature God, did not consider equality with God something to be grasped, but made himself nothing, taking the very nature of a servant, being made in human likeness. And being found in appearance as a man, he humbled himself and became obedient to death—even death on a cross!"

You know the rest of the story. Because of this humility, God raised Him up. We could add that because of this humility, humanity has raised Him up as well. Even people who won't call Him Lord acknowledge Him as a great teacher, human being, and leader.

Now here's the stinger. Paul introduces this hymn of praise to the humble Christ with this challenge: "Your attitude should be the same as that of Christ Jesus." If we are serious about becoming more Christlike, we must forget about self-assertion, power plays, and getting our own way. There is another way— a more humble way.

It is not a popular one though. Our society, after all, descends from ancient Greece and Rome. Humility was not touted among virtues of the Greeks. Pride gets the prize, not meekness. In ancient Rome, a conquering general did not return to the capital displaying his thanks to the gods and to his troops; rather, he paraded his booty and expected his countrymen's applause for his valor. He sallied forth to do battle *and* to return a hero. Praise was his goal and praise was his due.

Listen to our countrymen boasting "I did it my way." Hear them declaiming on what's "truth for me." Watch them scramble to "get what's coming to me." We're as dedicated to self-glory as any Roman general. Our dream is to live better than "they" do (whoever "they" are), rise higher than "they" can, and gain control in whatever circle we choose to enter. And in politics? Well, it's been a long time since a politician could legitimately refer to himself as "humble Abe." What we hear instead is, "If *I'm* elected, this is what *I* can do for you. Trust me. I'm the best."

As a young man, founding father Benjamin Franklin wrote his own self-improvement course. Twelve virtues, he decided, were necessary for the complete man. He would master each of them. Here's his list: temperance, silence, order, resolution, frugality, industry, sincerity, justice, moderation, cleanliness, tranquility, and chastity.

It's a good inventory, a worthwhile set of goals. Yet a Quaker friend let the determined overachiever know he had left something off: Franklin was often guilty of "pride," the friend said. Probably to Franklin's chagrin, his friend got specific, citing many examples of his propensity for being "overbearing and rather insolent." Stung by the rebuke but having to admit its justice, Franklin added a thirteenth virtue: "Humility: Imitate Jesus and Socrates."[1]

He didn't find the assignment an easy one, by the way. As an old man, he confessed that he couldn't "boast of much success in acquiring the *reality* of this virtue, but I had a good deal with regard to the *appearance* of it." He had learned that "there is perhaps no one of our natural passions so hard to subdue as pride; disguise it, struggle with it, beat it down, stifle it, mortify it as much as one pleases, it is still alive and will every now and then peep out and show itself." He further confessed that even if he had succeeded in overcoming his pride, he "would probably be proud of my humility."[2]

Franklin long has been acclaimed as one of the most influential leaders of the American Revolution. No one had more clout than he did, in part because more than any of his compatriots, he had "come down" to where the people were, and he never forgot them or considered himself above them. In contrast to many of his peers, he had no interest in becoming an aristocrat. He became, instead, the Great Commoner.

His is an example seldom followed by people in high places. Dan Rather's experience is typical. When the correspondent returned to Washington in 1966 from a journalistic tour of duty in Vietnam, Press Secretary Bill Moyers suggested Rather share his impressions of the war's progress (or lack of it) with President Lyndon Johnson. First, though, he wanted Rather to see Walt Rostow, the president's national security advisor.

A meeting was arranged. Rather had read and admired many of Rostow's writings and was impressed with his scholarly credentials. He was also a genial man. Rather was eager to meet with him because Moyers had left the impression that the administration wanted a fresh viewpoint. After spending a year on the battlefield mingling with American and Vietnamese service personnel, Rather had some things to report.

He didn't get to. To his surprise, Rostow was not interested. Instead, he proceeded to brief Rather, who picked up a number of inaccuracies in the report. Rostow said the situation was encouraging. "Good uses of armor." Rather had been there and had seen for himself that our forces had long since abandoned the use of armor. Rostow also claimed we were not bombing on the Cambodian side of the border. Rather had observed that bombing raids crossed the border daily.

"Once or twice I disagreed with Rostow. He did not like my comments. His attitude was not quite haughty. But he made it plain. 'This is the White House and this is the way it is.' And I retorted, in effect, 'That's fine. You're the ones with the map. But I just came from there. I was on the ground. And I know what I saw.'"

After the interview Rather reflected on the recommendation he did not make. He had become convinced that monthly, or at least once every three months, the president should order 100 company commanders to Washington from Vietnam and let them sit down with the commander-in-chief and tell him what was going on. He said he had never known a single person in any branch of the military "below the rank of colonel" to lie to him. He couldn't say the same for the top brass. They may have thought they were telling the truth, but they didn't know the truth. They wouldn't come down to learn it.[3]

## Come Down to Where the Living Is Easier

Coming down is not only the best way to learn what the people know; it is also a way of simplifying life. This may seem to be a strange conclusion to draw from the life of Jesus. For Him to come down entailed volunteering for the struggles of human existence. That hardly seems like the road to easy living.

I didn't say *easy* living, but *easier*. And for this principle I am not drawing as much on the example of Jesus as on His teaching in Matthew 11:28-30. These are some of Jesus' most popular words. They have comforted distressed men and women of every generation.

Ordinary people with average incomes often dream that if only they had more money, more clout, more of this world's goods, more freedom—you know, like the Kennedys and Fords and Rockefellers—life would be much easier. Compare the life of Microsoft CEO Bill Gates, for example, with Joe Mechanic or Sally Schoolteacher. They labor for every dollar, stretch it to cover the bills, moonlight to scrape up a few more dollars, and scramble for job security or possible advancement. And they dream of Gates's wealth. Would they trade places with him? In a heartbeat. Would they find life easier? It's doubtful.

Jesus is talking about something quite different from their daydreams:

> Come to me, all you who are weary and burdened,
> and I will give you rest. Take my yoke upon you
> and learn from me, for I am gentle and humble in
> heart, and you will find rest for your souls. For my
> yoke is easy and my burden is light
> (Matthew 11:28-30).

The issue for Jesus isn't income or lifestyle, but an entirely different life-*stance*. What He offers is quite the opposite of most "how to succeed" advice. He locates the source of anxiety and discouragement not in one's checkbook but in one's character. In place of pride and ambition, He prescribes gentleness and humility. Rather than scratching to get what's coming, He recommends teaming up with himself, which means doing His work, living like Him, and letting Him do the heavy hauling. He would have us banish pride. I've often jokingly asked people if they've ever considered "how much fun you could have if you had no pride at all."

It is a joke. A person with no self-regard is to be pitied. But so is the person with too much. A proud person finds that life is very difficult. The prideful are under severe pressure to keep up appearances, to be certain no one gets ahead of them, to guarantee they get everything that's coming to them. They must answer every insult, avenge every slight, carry every grudge, and take advantage of every opportunity to get even or get ahead. There is no rest for their souls.

On this one, Jesus did set the example for us: "Didn't you know I had to be in my Father's house?" It's the Father's opinion of Him that matters. When you become serious about becoming more like Jesus, you discover this exhilarating new freedom. Your critics and opponents will still beset you, but they will have no power over you. Through the din of their criticism, you'll be listening for one voice only. His approval is all you'll need. And that's liberating. This freedom is granted only to the humble.

# Come Down to Where Life Is Worth Living

You probably haven't been advised to go this direction before, certainly not on television. Commercials, to the contrary, beckon us to come *up* to better living. But now, after the multiplying scandals on Wall Street, in CEO offices, and among the glamorous people, you would think that the rest of us would be catching on. Maybe it's not quite as good as it seems up there.

When I read or watch ads pitching the "good life," I can't help thinking of the men and women who have come for counseling to find some escape *from* it. These aren't people life has passed by, the cruelly labeled "losers." No, these are the winners. They've driven themselves to the top of their professions. They've made big money and wield enormous power. They've moved "uptown."

And they don't like it. The burden has become too heavy. That kind of life, they have discovered to their dismay, costs too much. It isn't worth the price. They want a life, not just a livelihood.

So they come to their minister to talk about a career change. To borrow Bob Buford's excellent book title, in midlife they want to move "from success to significance." They want a new calling.

The apostle Paul addresses this calling in Ephesians 4:1-3. Once again his language is surprising. This significance, this worthwhileness, will not be gained through any of the usual high-powered stratagems of the fast track. Paul prescribes exactly the opposite. He begins where this books begins—with coming down.

> As a prisoner for the Lord, then, I urge you to live a life worthy of the calling you have received. Be completely humble and gentle; be patient, bearing with one another in love. Make every effort to keep the unity of the Spirit through the bond of peace.

Paul assumes you want Christ to guide your life. He further assumes you want your life to be worth the living. As far as he is concerned, the two are the same. To live like Jesus is to live with significance. This means you begin—you knew this was coming—by giving up your pride. Think of the proud people you have known. Would you call them gentle, patient, forbearing, dedicated to unity and peace? No way. They are the pushers, the demanders, the disturbers of the peace. They are dedicated to the preservation and promotion of their own causes.

No "coming down" for them.

But then, at the end of a lifetime of self-serving, what do they have that they can take with them? And who cares that they are gone?

## Come Down to Where You Are for God— and God Is for You

"A Savior has been born to you" (Luke 2:11). *To you.*

The Christmas story draws us back again and again because we believe that somehow, even though we can't easily explain the miracle, it's about *us*. The angels' announcement to the shepherds is as timely as ever. The Savior has come—for *us*.

Humbling yourself is ordinarily very difficult, even impossible—unless you think there's something in it for you. Humbling yourself before the one who loves you, who is *for you*, just makes sense.

In the text for the next chapter, Jesus explains to His worried parents that He had to be doing His Father's business.

For Him, the issue at hand was clear. He wasn't in the temple to show off, a child prodigy bedazzling His elders. Jesus was simply acting out as a youth what He would demonstrate and teach repeatedly as an adult. Give yourself to doing God's will, humbly and obediently, and God will take care of you. The teaching continues in the writings of Paul, as we have just noted, and is also in James:

> But he gives us more grace. That is why Scripture says:
>
> "God opposes the proud but gives grace to the humble."
>
> Submit yourselves, then, to God. Resist the devil, and he will flee from you. Come near to God and he will come near to you. Wash your hands, you sinners, and purify your hearts, you double-minded. Grieve, mourn and wail. Change your laughter to mourning and your joy to gloom. *Humble yourselves before the Lord, and he will lift you up* (4:6-10, italics mine).

To us proud self-asserters who insist on having our own way, everything's a struggle. Everybody's against us. It sometimes seems as if God himself is against us. "God, how can You do this to me?" we ask. Or we say, "Yo, Lord, it's me, and I got things for You to do for me. Can't You hear me?"

Note James's bluntness. There's a contest for your soul. Only one combatant can win. Either God will get you or the devil will. Go to the devil and see what you get. Go to God, and you get the worthwhile life, the easy burden, and significance.

Here's the difference. When friends leave you for a while, you say good-bye. That's short for "God be with you." You are asking a blessing on your friends. You want the best for them.

You never say, "The devil be with you." (At least I hope you don't. You'll quickly be pretty short of friends if you do.)

The truth is, we can't think anything better to wish a friend than "God be with you." The angels couldn't either.

# 2
# Built to Grow

## Luke 2:41-52

{
His mother treasured all these things in
her heart. And Jesus grew in wisdom and
stature, and in favor with God and men
(Luke 2:51, 52).
}

First Jesus came down. Then He grew up. We began with
humility because without this quality, spiritual growth won't
happen. Humility leads to obedience, obedience to learning,
learning to growth, and growth to character. But humility by
itself leads nowhere. Taking your place in the lowest instead of
the highest seats, or at the back instead of the front of the line,
or behind the spotlight instead of in it, doesn't mean a thing if
that's all you do. If, after humbling yourself, you don't grow
up, you'll just stay back there at the end of the line. You were
built for growth.

## What Does Obeying Have to Do with Growing?

A prince in a feeding trough—this is the central image of
Jesus' birth story. The boy amidst the temple teachers—this is
our picture of Jesus' youth.

> Every year his parents went to Jerusalem for the
> Feast of the Passover. When he was twelve years
> old, they went up to the Feast, according to the
> custom. After the Feast was over, while his parents
> were returning home, the boy Jesus stayed
> behind in Jerusalem, but they were unaware of it.
> Thinking he was in their company, they traveled
> on for a day. Then they began looking for him
> among their relatives and friends. When they
> did not find him, they went back to Jerusalem to
> look for him. After three days they found him in
> the temple courts, sitting among the teachers,
> listening to them and asking them questions
> (Luke 2:41-46).

My Sunday school memories of this passage are pretty dim.
The part I remember most vividly comes later:

> Everyone who heard him was amazed at his
> understanding and his answers. When his parents
> saw him, they were astonished. His mother said
> to him, "Son, why have you treated us like this?
> Your father and I have been anxiously searching
> for you."
>
> "Why were you searching for me?" he asked.
> "Didn't you know I had to be in my Father's
> house?" But they did not understand what he was
> saying to them (Luke 2:47-50).

I don't know whether it was because my teachers stressed
Jesus' obedience in doing His Father's business, or because
I was so impressed that a 12-year-old could amaze the temple
teachers, but in my recollections the emphasis has always
been on Jesus' brilliance. Only a boy, He was instructing the
instructors.

I must have skipped over the earlier verses. There, in verse 46, we find Him "sitting among the teachers, listening . . . asking them questions." Ah! Before He taught, He studied. Before amazing them, He was their obedient student.

The Scriptures present tantalizingly few glimpses of Jesus' childhood and youth. Although some apocryphal stories of a miracle-working Savior-child circulated after He was gone, they lacked credibility and were excluded from the scriptural canon. As far as the Bible is concerned, Jesus led a normal home life, undoubtedly underwent the usual storms and stresses of maturation, and learned at the feet of His mother Mary and at the bench of His carpenter father Joseph. He had, like the rest of us, a lot to learn, so He didn't rush into His ministry but waited until He was 30. By then, His personal growth had prepared Him.

In our day of instant expertise, Jesus' humility and gradual maturation offer refreshing relief. Radio and television gurus spout instant advice to the confused, often before the problem is even fully posed. They have no doubts, no hesitations, only simplistic solutions delivered on the spot. Where did they come from, these celebrity authorities? How did they prepare? With whom have they studied? Have they immersed themselves in the real issues or did they study just enough to impress the audience?

*A word of warning here*: I'm not suggesting that academic degrees guarantee a person's expertise. People who have earned a doctorate, for instance, are usually much less impressed by their accomplishment than people who haven't earned one. The doctorate title merely indicates that the bearer has completed a certain course of studies and fulfilled requirements for the degree. It is no guarantee of either mastery of a body of knowledge or attainment of wisdom along the way. No one is more pitiful than a pompous Dr. So-and-So who believes that the title makes him or her somehow better than other people.

Jesus' modesty in the temple is appealing. He understands that before the teaching comes the learning. Before the commanding comes the obeying.

## When Does Obeying Look Like Disobeying?

In the last chapter I quoted Benjamin Franklin. The latest biography about him contains another bit of insight. He had discovered that some white people preferred living like the Native Americans to living like their own kind. He noted that when white children were captured and raised by Native Americans and then later returned to white society, "in a short time they become disgusted with our manner of life, and the care and pains that are necessary to support it, and take the first good opportunity of escaping again into the woods." Were they disobedient and rebellious? Or had they simply chosen to obey different teachers?

Franklin also told of some Massachusetts commissioners who provided free education at Harvard for a dozen young Native Americans. Native American elders turned down the offer though. They said they had sent some of their young braves to study there years earlier, but it wasn't good for them. When they returned they were "neither acquainted with the true methods for killing deer, catching beaver, or surprising the enemy." The Native Americans didn't want their young men so disqualified for success in life. Franklin reported they offered instead "to educate a dozen or so white children in the ways of the Indians 'and make men of them.'"[4]

From the Native American parents' point of view, their Harvard-educated children were no longer obedient to the ways of their people. They had, instead, learned the white man's ways. What qualified them in one society disqualified them in another; what appeared to be obedience in one looked like disobedience in the other.

This same clash of expectations informs this story. Were Joseph and Mary pleased that Jesus remained in the temple while they returned home? When they discovered His absence and had to retrace their steps to Jerusalem in search of Him, was their first reaction to praise Him? Or were they, as most parents would have been, distraught, perhaps panicky, and more than a little perturbed that He had disobeyed—if not their explicit demand that He stay with the group, then their assumption that He would? Were they satisfied with His explanation or did He seem impertinent? ("Didn't you know I had to be in my Father's house?") Luke says they didn't understand. Did they approve?

This chapter is considering the role of obedience in character development. If we do not heed our teachers, we will not learn what they have to teach us. Obedience is essential in the learning process. But obedience to whom? And when? Jesus was obeying His heavenly Father, but an outside observer may well have thought He was being disobedient, or at least disrespectful, to His parents. Which was it?

When young Thomas Aquinas announced his decision to become a Benedictine monk, his parents were so upset they locked him up for a couple of years until he repented, which he never did. They finally relented and released him. He went on to become perhaps the most influential Christian of the high Middle Ages. When Francis of Assisi decided to renounce his family's wealth and become a poor friar, he also had to withstand the wrath of his incredulous father. Sometimes obedience looks like disobedience.

My parents supported my decision to become a minister. When I left home to prepare, however, I met many young men and women who were pursuing theological studies even though their parents disapproved and, in some cases, disowned them for doing so. As far as their parents were concerned, they were rebellious children. Their obedience to their calling looked like disobedience to their parents.

Character is built on humility and obedience. The question is not whether we will obey, but whom. "You cannot serve God and money," Jesus will later teach. You will choose; you will serve. When you make your choice, be prepared for the consequences. A Christian cannot expect to obey Jesus' teaching without looking weird, even rebellious, to the worldly. Like Jesus' parents, they will not understand.

## When Does the Student Become the Teacher?

Let me repeat what I wrote earlier: By then His personal growth had prepared Him. At 30, Jesus was ready to begin. Have you ever wondered when you will be ready? When will you have been obedient enough and studied enough to presume to teach others? Jesus "grew in wisdom and stature, and in favor with God and men" (Luke 2:52). These words were written of a 12-year-old. Yet 18 more years elapsed before He took up His calling. Not until then was the time ripe to teach.

Pondering that Sunday school memory verse as a senior adult raises other questions. When do we stop growing, learning, preparing? When is it *safe* to stop? When can we feel comfortable with our intellectual and spiritual achievements? When can we feel confident enough to teach?

My Sunday school teachers urged us to keep on growing intellectually ("in wisdom") just as we would grow in stature (some of us were more successful here than others). We were to protect and enhance our reputations for Christ's sake ("in favor with . . . men") and grow ever closer to God's will for us ("in favor with God"). This sounded like a reasonable set of goals in my youth. Is it a reasonable set for an adult drawing a Social Security check? When is enough growth enough?

Another question for the elderly. As retired persons, we are generally without titles or position or influence. There is no doubt that we are less highly regarded by man ("and in favor with . . . men"). But with God? Does He who sees the inner person value us less because the outer symbols of success have disappeared? Does He expect us to keep on growing, even as our energy wanes and attention spans shorten?

Even more to the point, *can* we keep growing? A child has the young Jesus to guide him. An adult has the mature Jesus to guide her. But a senior adult? Is the character of Jesus at 30 what we should be growing toward at 70? Is it possible to retain the flexibility and enthusiasm for adventure, which learning requires, at this stage of life?

These are questions this writer can't answer from personal experience. I can offer a few comments about young old age, but about extreme old age, when just keeping the body functioning becomes a full-time job, I can't. I can offer a few examples, though, of men and women who apparently never seemed to view themselves as having arrived, but instead kept learning, thinking, and sharing what they learned.

Just one example will have to suffice. Orrin Root, a senior editor at Standard Publishing, died in 2003 at the age of 98. Although only a relatively small number of the people he influenced attended his funeral, thousands more would feel the loss of this quiet man. He retired from his full-time editing position more than three decades earlier, yet Standard Publishing wouldn't let him quit. The editorial department kept calling him back. When he died, he was still writing a weekly column for *The Lookout* (a Standard Publishing magazine)—and was months ahead of his deadlines—and continuing to do special jobs for the company. To be able to produce as he did required constant study. He had to keep checking his sources, rethinking his positions, then writing with the authority that only years of maturing could offer.

If you had asked Orrin Root when a person was old enough to stop learning, he would have told you he didn't know. He wasn't there yet. A teacher he had become long ago, but a student he remained until the very end.

## What Does Religion Have to Do with Growth?

Jesus' session with the temple teachers raises another interesting issue—the importance of religious observance. The family had gone to Jerusalem to fulfill the requirements of their religion. Later, as an adult, Jesus observed the rituals of His people's faith. He was never casual about religion, even when His critics thought He was.

I recently participated in a meeting of college and university administrators. There was nothing "religious" on the agenda, yet as the meeting progressed, the topic turned to spiritual matters. Several participants took pains to separate themselves from religion while insisting they were quite spiritual. I may have been the only person there who was uncomfortable. My discomfort stemmed from their casual use of *spiritual*, a term applied so broadly today it no longer means much. *God* also seemed to be whatever they wanted him (or her or it) to be. They evidenced no rootedness in Scripture and little or no concern for the traditions of their religious heritage. They spoke mostly of their feelings. They clearly were not "about their Father's business" but about their own. They were on self-directed, self-administered, self-evaluated courses of self-improvement covered with a façade of acceptable "spirituality," but without the disciplines of formal religion.

They are admirable men and women, dedicated public servants genuinely concerned about the welfare of their students. They are also persons of moral rectitude. They can be trusted. Many of them, however, have had negative experiences in church. They want a spiritual life free of religious traditionalism.

In this respect they are not far from Jesus, who had so much to say about the yeast of the Pharisees and the corruptions of corporate religious life. The difference is that He nevertheless submitted himself as a child and later as an adult to the disciplines of the faith. When He departed from the norm, it was not in rebellion but in order to rescue the faith from the legalists. His primary concern was not His personal spiritual life but His mission to seek and save the lost. He who required a disciplined life of His followers first modeled that discipline for them.

In the discussions, my thoughts drifted again to Jesus. Like my fellow educators, I have to confess that I'm uncomfortable with many of the trappings of religion. Unlike some of them, though, I'm not convinced I can improve on my heritage. For certain, I have no doubt that I cannot improve on the character of Jesus. So I too want to be about my Father's business. In my case, that means learning at the feet of this one who, as a 12-year-old, first listened to and then taught the temple teachers.

## When Does the Growing Get Easier?

Not long ago I received two similar e-mails on the same day. They were both from young ministerial associates of mine. Each wanted some advice about pursuing more education. They had proven themselves as students and as ministers. They could coast and still perform respectably. But something was driving them to learn more. They believed that by going for their doctorates, they would be more highly qualified and, simply put, do a better job.

I'm proud of them. They want to keep growing, so they will have to submit to the necessary disciplines. They have families to provide for. They will have to juggle the demands of home, church, and school. It won't be easy. But it will be worth it.

They will not have Malcolm Muggeridge's epitaph on their grave marker. Shortly after his college days at Cambridge University, Muggeridge, who later went on to fame and fortune in journalism, wrote his own epitaph and sent it to a friend: "Here lieth one whose soul sometimes burned with great longings. To whom sometimes the curtain of the Infinite was opened just a little, but who lacked the guts to make any use of it."[5]

For many years he wrestled with his spiritual impulses, even as he soared ever higher in his remarkable career. Finally, he admitted to himself, his friends, and his worldwide audience that he was becoming a Christian. He at last had "the guts" to make use of his great longings and obey Christ. I suspect that obedience never became easy for this driven, high-maintenance personality.

My hope for my two correspondents is that they will be like Muggeridge. They are strong-willed, independent-thinking men with great longings. They have peeked through the curtain of the infinite. They are ready for a closer look.

That "look" won't consist only of amassing more information. At their stage of growth, further education isn't so much about expanding one's database as it is about clarifying values and arriving at simplicity. To learn is to eliminate as much as it is to accumulate. We are frequently told that the average man or woman has to process more information in a twenty-first-century day than a man or woman did in a sixteenth-century lifetime. Supposedly, knowledge is doubling every five years (although I can't help wondering how anyone measures it). That's too much for anyone to master.

My friends do not need a lot more information. They are seeking, instead, deeper insight into the infinite and a more faithful imitation of the character of Christ in this finite world. They take seriously John's injunction: "We know that we have come to know him if we obey his commands. The man who says, 'I know him,' but does not do what he commands is a liar, and the truth is not in him. But if anyone obeys his word, God's love is truly made complete in him. This is how we know we are in him: Whoever claims to live in him must walk as Jesus did" (1 John 2:3-6). They want to obey, to walk as He walked.

Their immediate model could be another friend of mine. Bob Russell is the senior minister of Southeast Christian Church in Louisville, Kentucky, one of the largest congregations in America. He is a role model for young preachers everywhere—and some of us older ones as well. If anybody appears to "have it made," to have completed the course in Christian growth and maturation, it is Bob. But if he's telling the truth (and I have never known him to do otherwise), it is not always easy for him to be obedient to his calling. He too still has to discipline himself. He has publicly confessed that sometimes:

- he has to force himself occasionally to go to church "because I'm commanded not to forsake the assembling of Christian people (Hebrews 10:25). I go to worship out of a sense of duty."

- he smiles at people when he arrives in a grumpy mood, "because I'm commanded, 'Be kind . . . to one another' (Ephesians 4:32). It's part of my duty to be kind."

- he sings when he doesn't feel like singing because the Scripture enjoins, "Speak to one another with psalms, hymns, and spiritual songs. Sing and make music in your heart to the Lord" (Ephesians 5:19). "It's my duty to sing."

- he preaches even though there are times that he'd rather not. He takes seriously the scriptural exhortation: "Preach the Word; be prepared in season and out of season; correct, rebuke and encourage—with great patience and careful instruction" (2 Timothy 4:2). Russell takes that to mean, "Preach whether it's popular or not; preach whether you feel like it or not."

Bob Russell has discovered something through this obedience though. "On these rare mornings that start so sour, I notice a pattern. When I 'discharge all the duties of [my] ministry,' my spirits almost always revive!"[6]

Of course. Obeying the right teacher leads to gladness. And growth.

# 3
# Built to Last

## Luke 4:1-13

{
Jesus . . . was led by the Spirit in
the desert, where for forty days he was
tempted by the devil. . . . When the
devil had finished all this tempting, he
left him until an opportune time
(Luke 4:1, 2, 13).
}

Perhaps this chapter should be titled "Built to Survive," since the TV reality rage has made survival shows so popular. The usual explanation for the phenomenon is that the viewing audience has wearied of contrived programs and wants something more natural, more "authentic"—although why people think that marooning a dozen publicity hounds on a deserted island and subjecting them to a series of extreme and often disgusting endurance tests can be considered realistic is a bit baffling. One faithful viewer explained she is drawn to them because they are about relationships, adventure, choices, and, yes, survival. She added that what she doesn't like is the conniving, "but that's life. It's what people do to survive."

While the artificial situations are patently phony, endurance testing is not. What is life if not a test? If it isn't, why do old people boast that only the strong (meaning themselves, of course) survive? How else can you explain that success often is threatening to people because they are certain it can't last? Things may be going well now but there's trouble ahead. They fear their endurance test is coming.

Synonyms for *tested* are revealing: experienced, veteran, hardened, weathered. Taken together, they all spell tough times. Experienced what? Difficulties, trials, challenges. Veteran of what? War (including, but by no means limited to, the military kind). Hardened? The soft do not make it. Weathered? Many, many storms.

I searched the thesaurus's synonyms for *test*. The one I was seeking may have had too moral a sound, smacking overly of the religious, to be included. At any rate, "tempted" wasn't mentioned. Jesus' endurance test is generally referred to as His temptation in the wilderness, not His survival test, but if He didn't pass this ordeal, He wouldn't be fit for the mission ahead.

## Jesus' Endurance Test

Jesus' wilderness trial, in which Bible scholars often find parallels with Moses' self-banishment from the royal court in Egypt or even with Israel's 40 years of wandering in the wilderness, goes to the core of human experience. Every pivotal temptation is a test of spiritual resistance. Am I strong enough, committed enough, to hold up? Will I be faithful in spite of the pressure to cave in? Evolutionists speak of the survival of the fittest. Pastors pray for the survival of the faithful. Will their flocks remain true to the Lord, to their church, to their highest ideals, in spite of the circling wolves of seduction? What is life itself if not an alluring—and threatening—wilderness of temptations? How can a normal person resist?

Jesus could not be immune if He was to be one of us. It is not coincidental that in Luke 4, at the start of Jesus' extraordinary ministry and right after God so dramatically affirmed Him at His baptism, Satan does his best to stop Jesus.

Even though we have read it many times before, this dramatic contest draws us back for another close reading. Each time we see something new, something we had not lived long enough to see earlier. Our own lengthening temptation history makes us appreciate Jesus' triumph all the more.

Luke tells the story without embellishment. We already know that Jesus is going to win. What makes us probe more deeply is that we want—we need—to know how He held up under an assault that would defeat most of us. Demons and monsters we can fight, but Jesus' struggle was against very desirable possibilities.

> Jesus, full of the Holy Spirit, returned from the Jordan and was led by the Spirit in the desert, where for forty days he was tempted by the devil. He ate nothing during those days, and at the end of them he was hungry.
>
> The devil said to him, "If you are the Son of God, tell this stone to become bread."
>
> Jesus answered, "It is written: 'Man does not live on bread alone.'"
>
> The devil led him up to a high place and showed him in an instant all the kingdoms of the world. And he said to him, "I will give you all their authority and splendor, for it has been given to me, and I can give it to anyone I want to. So if you worship me, it will all be yours."
>
> Jesus answered, "It is written: 'Worship the Lord your God and serve him only.'"

> The devil led him to Jerusalem and had him stand
> on the highest point of the temple. "If you are the
> Son of God," he said, "throw yourself down from
> here. For it is written:
>
> "'He will command his angels concerning you to
> guard you carefully; they will lift you up in their
> hands, so that you will not strike your foot against
> a stone.'"
>
> Jesus answered, "It says: 'Do not put the Lord your
> God to the test.'"
>
> When the devil had finished all this tempting, he
> left him until an opportune time (Luke 4:1-13).

You can understand why I looked up the relationship between testing and tempting, can't you? Jesus said, "Do not put the Lord your God to the *test*" [italics mine]. The next verse reads, "When the devil had finished all this *tempting . . .* " [italics mine]. Temptation *tests* the tempted. Jesus' preparation is undergoing its final inspection. No, that isn't quite accurate. It is the final inspection before His formal ministry begins, but as the last verse makes ominously clear, the devil isn't finished with Him yet: "He left him until an opportune time." He'll be back. He always comes back. Had Jesus had 40 years of ministry, the devil would still be back. Our tests continue right up to our final exam:

> When the Son of Man comes in his glory, and all
> the angels with him, he will sit on his throne in
> heavenly glory. All the nations will be gathered
> before him, and he will separate the people one
> from another as a shepherd separates the sheep
> from the goats (Matthew 25:31, 32).

Until that day, or the day when our bodies are returned to the dust, the testing continues. Will we be faithful? Will we be loyal? Will we have the power to resist the deepest destructive desires of our heart? We wish we could be certain.

What makes this episode in Jesus' life so unsettling is that the devil offers Him only what we all want, what we think we need, and what our culture insists we deserve. We are not bothered so much by the devil's attack as by our own vulnerability. If he were to offer us upstanding citizens of twenty-first-century America what he holds out to Jesus, could we tell him, "No thank you"? He urges Jesus to take exactly what we have been taught to demand for ourselves.

## Feed Yourself!

{ "If you are the Son of God, tell this stone to become bread" (Luke 4:3).

Why not? After Jesus fasted for more than a month, He was famished. He had received God's blessing on His ministry. How could it be wrong to use His power to quiet those incessant hunger pangs? Just a little bread, that's all He needed.

Go for it, Jesus! Your body has rights too, you know! Your walk with God may be spiritual, but you take that walk in a body and it needs to be strong. You won't be much good to anybody if your body breaks down. Take care of yourself first; then you'll be fit to help others. Feed *yourself.* Sound familiar?

To judge by bookstore shelves, grocery store racks, television commercials, and talk shows, our bodies are not just needy; they define us. You don't like the definition? Have it reconstructed. Straighten the nose, lift the eyebrows, rebuild the jaw, round out the buttocks, lengthen the legs, transplant the hair, implant the breasts, and fatten the lips. The current you is unattractive. The way to a new, delectable you is to remodel your body. Feed *yourself*.

Don't overlook diet and exercise either. The media are ringing all kinds of alarms today over Americans' growing obesity. We're too fat. We're also too lazy. We eat too much and exercise too little. So a multibillion-dollar industry has grown up to serve the body. How many diet control books and programs are on the market now? We lose count. The same has to be said for health spas and exercise parlors and bodybuilding equipment. Television's Dr. Phil is personally leading a crusade to wipe out obesity. You must pay attention to your physique. You can't help others if you don't help yourself first. Feed *yourself*.

Proper care also entails fully expressing yourself sexually. In this liberated age, sexual freedom is your basic right. How can you hear others' cries for help when your libido is screaming for satisfaction? Our Victorian predecessors were wrong. You can't suppress the drive. A healthy not-to-be-denied sex life makes for a healthier you. Your body must be served. Feed *yourself*.

And then there's pain. The apostle Paul may write about beating his body and making it his slave (1 Corinthians 9:26, 27), but his modern descendant reaches for the medicine cabinet. Drugs, when used properly, may be helpful. But when they become the master and the user the slave, "Feed *yourself*" can be a prescription for self-destruction.

If this scene were being enacted in your town today, do you think the devil might put a little different spin on the temptation to turn stones into bread? Rural residents may still make their own bread, but most of us head for the supermarket or nearest bakery. Of course, we can't buy it without money. It's no wonder that *bread* is often synonymous with money. You pay for your bread with your "bread." When we ask the Lord to "give us this day our daily bread," we don't just mean baked flour; we mean the necessities of life that we purchase with money. The body doesn't just have to eat; it needs "bread" to buy the food, the exercise equipment, the drugs, the sexual opportunities, or whatever else we've convinced ourselves that we need. The devil wouldn't find it too difficult to trap us on this very first temptation, would he? He could just whisper, "Feed *yourself!*"

## Empower Yourself!

"I will give you all their [the kingdoms of the world's] authority and splendor, for it has been given to me, and I can give it to anyone I want to. So if you worship me, it will all be yours" (Luke 4:6).

This is the power test. It goes by different names. For Americans, it's claiming the promise enshrined in the Declaration of Independence: the right to "Life, Liberty and the pursuit of Happiness." We call it self-governance, being yourself, or doing your own thing (and what's more, doing it *my* way).

There's a very short distance between claiming the power to do what you want and demanding that other people do what you want. It isn't just ownership of lands and nations that the devil offers Jesus; it is "authority and splendor." Authority over what? Splendor as judged by whom? The issue of power quickly shifts from mere dominion over things to domination over people. The media's insistence that you deserve to spoil yourself ("after all, I'm worth it") leaves out the inevitable con-sequence. For you to get everything you want sooner or later deprives someone else for your sake.

When my wife Joy and I toured the magnificent antebellum homes and plantations of the pre-Civil War South, we admired the workmanship of the houses and grounds and oohed and aahed over the elegance and civility of society in those days. For inspiration, southern aristocrats drew heavily on the courts and Europe; at great expense, they transported transatlantic grandeur to America. These wealthy men and women exercised enormous power over their little kingdoms. But their kingdoms rode on the backs of their powerless slaves. It was a rotten elegance.

I couldn't help wondering, as we walked through these monuments to past splendor, how much power is enough? Lord Acton recognized that "power tends to corrupt and absolute power corrupts absolutely." How much power can we assume before healthy personal independence twists into tyranny?

The temptation, as we noted above, is power, but that is not really the issue here, as both the devil and Jesus know. What the devil wants is Jesus' worship. And that is exactly what Jesus will not give him.

He does not defeat the devil through self-assertion or by measuring His own strength against the devil's. What could have turned into a titanic power struggle between the two of them is quietly deflected by Jesus' reliance on an even higher power: "Worship the Lord your God and serve him only" (Luke 4:8).

Remarkably, Jesus maintains this attitude throughout His ministry. Even at the height of His popularity, He refuses to let the people stampede Him into higher office, or entice Him to use His miraculous powers for personal gain. He employs them only to heal, never to hurt or demean. He won't even let himself be called "good," but insists that God, whom He worships, is the only good one—the only one deserving to be worshiped. As the apostle Paul later marveled, "he humbled himself and became obedient to death—even death on a cross" (Philippians 2:8). A modern disciple of Jesus can't help wondering what He would think of our incessant clamoring for our rights (our *powers*). For certain, He wouldn't have joined the clamorers.

For Jesus, worship of the Father eliminated any need to build a power base for himself. The Father's strength was enough.

One of the most influential men of the twentieth century was Mahatma Gandhi of India. Although he remained a Hindu, he drew inspiration from the life of Christ and, in many ways, sought to imitate Him. In nothing did he follow Jesus' example more than in his application of power. As a young man, former Secretary of State Dean Rusk heard Gandhi speak at Oxford University in England. Gandhi was just out of an English prison, where he had been incarcerated for resisting British authority in India. He sat cross-legged in his loincloth on a table at the front of the room, fielding questions. Nearby were the two goats that he kept for their milk, his principal food. At that session Rusk learned the secret of Gandhi's remarkable power—the secret ingredient of the formula that would eventually break England's grip on the subcontinent. "We Indians cannot expel the British by returning their fire gun-for-gun, cannon-for-cannon. We simply don't have the means. But we can drive them out of India because they can't stay there without us. All we have to do is sit down. Now some of us may starve; some of us may die. But the British will have to leave. That is raw power."[7]

As you know, Jesus employed this same strategy, what we have come to call passive resistance. He paid the price as Gandhi and many of his followers would. However, His primary objective wasn't to save His own life but to save the lives of others. The struggle was not about Him but about us. He would not be enticed or forced to defend himself. Bolstered by Scripture and indwelt by the Holy Spirit, He could withstand the devil's wiles because He had access to greater power than the devil offered. The devil could kill Him, but even death could not defeat His mission. Gandhi was right. That is raw power.

## Express Yourself!

> The devil led him to Jerusalem and had him stand on the highest point of the temple. "If you are the Son of God," he said, "throw yourself down from here. For it is written:
>
> "'He will command his angels concerning you to guard you carefully; they will lift you up in their hands, so that you will not strike your foot against a stone'" (Luke 4:9-11).

Why might Jesus be tempted by this final challenge? Because He could be, that's why. You and I couldn't. This would be no temptation for us. God has never promised angels to keep us from hurting ourselves when we do something outrageous. No way is anybody going to get us to jump off the highest building. We're not that stupid.

Not *that* stupid, but maybe a little stupid. We are quite willing to show off in other ways. That's really what the devil is trying to get Jesus to do. "Show your stuff, Jesus!" he taunts. "You think You're so special. Prove it."

Not long ago, Joy and I visited New York's Guggenheim Museum because of its renowned architect, Frank Lloyd Wright. She had never been there; I had first visited it in the fifties, then again many years later. The building, so elegantly simple and marvelously impractical, still fascinates, though it is now a little weathered. The exhibit that day, though of course different from my earlier visits, was a reminder that even the Guggenheim doesn't always show good artistic taste.

At least to this amateur's eye. On display were giant canvases of a famous expressionist. Expressionism is a school of art that I have diligently tried to appreciate but don't. The artist is not offering his "impressions" of the world, as the French impressionists do, for example. His purpose is to express himself. What he offers may or may not make sense, may or may not have any point of contact with the viewer. That doesn't matter. The painting reveals the artist's peculiar perspective; his reference point is not reality as others see it, but as he sees it. He has expressed himself. Take it or leave it. It is art at its most self-centered—the artist doing what he wants to because he can.

"Come on, Jesus. Throw yourself down. You can. God will take care of You," the devil says as he tries to tempt Jesus. How easily trust in God slips into abuse of God. From worship of God to worship of self. From praising God to using God for one's own purposes. From striving for Christlike character to expressing one's "true" self. Spend some time with a self-expressionist; you'll walk away wondering how self-expression differs from what we used to call selfishness and how selfishness differs from self-worship. You'll be hard-pressed to find the difference.

When the trial was over, the devil had done his best, but his best wasn't good (or bad) enough. His victim rejected the bait. The tempter lost.

## Jesus—Faithful *and* Victorious

So far we have only hinted at the obvious. Luke makes certain we don't miss it: throughout the temptations, he says,

47

Jesus was "full of the Holy Spirit." He drew on strength greater than His own.

Unlike Martin Scorsese's Jesus in the infamous movie, *The Last Temptation of Christ*, Luke's Jesus is not like a man at the end of His resources, emaciated from fasting and inner torment, reeling on the precipice of despair and unconsciousness. How could anyone be drawn to become a disciple of such an effete Jesus? When you read Luke's account, on the other hand, two strong emotions sweep over you: the first is unabashed admiration. With nothing more than the sword of Scripture and the Spirit of God, Jesus defeats the devil. No "wimp factor" here. This is somebody you want to follow.

The second emotion is embarrassment. Jesus is the protagonist in this story, but it's about you and me as much as it is about Him. The triumphal part belongs to Jesus, certainly, but the temptation parts are our story. Could you have held out as well as He did? I couldn't have. I don't have His command of Scriptures; my "sword" is rusty from disuse, my commitment to mission wobbly. And although I also have the promised Holy Spirit, I am not accomplished in availing myself of this power. If I'm to achieve anything like Jesus' victory, I need to become much more like Him in drawing on these resources.

The good news is that becoming more like Him is something you and I can do. We also want to remember that "triumph" is not demanded of us, but we can't be satisfied with mere survival either. Jesus did more than survive. He overcame. The devil turned his heaviest guns on Him, but Jesus did not fall.

His was a colossal victory.

That's what His achievement looks like to us, anyway. I suspect, though, that Jesus would find my language inflated. When it was all over, He was exhausted. No victory celebration for Him. To our knowledge, He never later boasted about that time when He bested the devil in mortal combat. As far as Jesus was concerned, He was simply being faithful.

That's all He asks of us as well. And the resources that were His—the Word of the Lord and the indwelling of the Holy Spirit—are ours as well. Drawing on them, we can stand up to the devil himself.

We just have to be faithful. And that we can do.

# 4
# Built to Care

### Luke 7:11-17

When the Lord saw her, his heart
went out to her and he said, "Don't cry"
(Luke 7:13).

So far we have discussed three of Jesus' characteristics we want to imitate: humility, obedience, and faithfulness to His mission. We have followed the order of Luke's account of Jesus' birth, youth, and early ministry. With this chapter we come to the quality that, perhaps more than any other, explains His amazing hold on people's affection. One brief clause says it all: "His heart went out to her." He reacts to the grief of a bereaved widow with the compassion that typifies all His dealings with hurting people.

## Understanding Jesus' "Heart Talk"

Luke's language is the kind you don't hear much when guys are talking. It sounds a little too wimpy for man-talk. Women's hearts may go out, but men's usually don't. They think that's what women do just before they burst into tears, and real men don't cry—at least, so the men of my generation were taught; younger ones seem to have permission to be a little freer with their emotions.

For males my age, anyway, this "heart talk" smacks too much of all the pop psychology that has been dumped on us in recent years, all those exhortations to get in touch with "your feminine side," to let your feelings out. Show some sympathy, they urge us. Don't be so left-brained (your logical, rational side). Give your right brain (your intuitive, empathetic side) a chance. It isn't always what you think, they say, but more often what you feel that's important. You left-brainers are always explaining, barking orders, and taking charge. Let's have a little more touchy-feely here.

At least, that's how it sounds and feels to a lot of men. So you won't hear us saying something like, "My heart goes out to you," even when it does.

And it does. We won't utter the words, but our hearts go out anyway. We might be more comfortable with the now obsolete language of the *King James Version* of the Bible. What Luke calls "heart" was often translated "bowels," as in "bowels of mercy." The seat of human emotions has moved upward from the bowels to the heart since the *King James Version* was published in 1611. So the next time you hear a man say, "It took guts to do that," pay attention. He may not just be referring to some courageous act of daring. He may actually be speaking of someone being moved by bowels of mercy ("his heart went out to her") to do the loving thing even when he risks being thought a sissy by his peers.

How else can you explain the heroism so much in evidence on and after September 11, 2001, in New York and Washington, D.C.? Or the rescue workers digging out men buried alive in mine shafts? Or parents working overtime to be certain their children have enough to eat and a chance for a better life than their own? Or medical workers who forget all about the clock as they fight to bring someone back from the edge? It's not an issue of right brain versus left brain, or modern language versus now obsolete terminology. It's about having a heart (or the bowels).

We're talking love here. Not the Valentine's Day variety and certainly not just hormone-driven human coupling, but love that spots a grieving woman in a crowd, feels her pain, and does something about it. *Agape*, the New Testament word for the highest kind of love, is both right- and left-brained. It's rational action (left brain) energized by deep feeling (right). It's thought-plus-feeling-plus-action. When the heart is moved, something good happens.

Recently some very good friends of ours lost their 24-year-old granddaughter in a car accident. The young woman, a dental student in Portland, Oregon, had gone to my hometown of Tillamook to spend a little time with her family. Driving back to her school, she fell asleep at the wheel. Her death was instantaneous, the only blessing in this otherwise tragic happening. We hardly knew what to say to our friends. Unfortunately, they had been there before. It seemed like only yesterday, yet it was 20 years ago that they had buried a son. In another automobile accident, only this time with a drunk driver at the wheel, their high school son was killed as he was jogging along the road with some friends.

Do I have to tell you how our hearts "went out to" them? We too have buried a son. And an adoptive grandson. We grieved for them as we had earlier grieved for ourselves.

Jesus didn't have to be told what the widow felt. He knew.

*Empathy* is the word for this ability to identify with the pain of another. It goes beyond sympathy, which shows pity for the

plight of another; empathy feels it as if it were its own. It is what
Dr. Hacib Aouan describes in the *Annals of Internal Medicine*.
Dr. Aouan contracted AIDS when a blood-filled capillary tube
fractured and cut one of his fingers. His patient was a teenager
with leukemia who had received many transfusions without
incident, but the blood of this tube was tainted. The accident happened five years before Dr. Aouan described his life-altering experience. He had always been the doctor; now he was the patient.
This reversal gave him new insight into the physician's role:

> A good doctor goes through the struggle of an
> illness with you, providing support while protecting
> your dignity and independence, and searches
> constantly for better options for your care. . . .
> As a patient I have learned that just as important
> as medical expertise and the proper use of new
> technologies is the ability of the physician to show
> legitimate concern, to be there during the bad
> times, and to provide hope even to the incurable.[8]

Now afflicted with AIDS, Dr. Aouan has learned what no
amount of medical training could teach him about the help-
lessness, the fear, the dependency, the loss of dignity, and the
desperate search for a reason to keep hoping that haunt other
patients. He has learned something about compassion.


## Growing in Compassion

This is the only chapter in this book that comforts as much
as it challenges me. The others hold up lofty ideals that in my
case are yet to be achieved. I seem so far from having reached
the goal. On the subject of compassion, however, I am encour-
aged. I can honestly say I've made discernible progress. I am a
more caring person than I was 40 years ago.

Not that I can take any credit for the progress. I wish I could tell you that I have discovered 10 proven principles for developing a more compassionate character. I haven't. No, I have simply lived long enough to have been hurt badly enough to genuinely feel others' pain as I couldn't when I was young, ambitious, combative, and terribly certain I was right (and woe to anyone who doubted me).

But now with careers behind me and grandchildren multiplying around Joy and me, I've personally and socially experienced enough of this world's pain not to want anybody else to have to experience it. I've seen too many wars, too many famines, too many divorces, too many accidents, too many personal tragedies, too much poverty, too many sick and dying children, too many broken dreams, too many widows losing their only sons.

There's a very old story of a man who dies and goes to Heaven. Upon arriving, he is shown into God's office in which an enormous window looks out over the earth. While he waits, the man stands at the window drinking in the scene. Wonder fills him as he studies the planet's beauty—its blue waters, green forests, and white clouds. That's his first impression. But the longer he looks, the more he sees. His initial wonder vanishes. Now he's surveying the devastation wrought by human selfishness and greed, the ravages of war, and the unbridled exploitation of the planet's resources. He can't look any longer. He turns away muttering that if he were God, he'd blast the earth out of the sky and start over.

But then a voice behind him says, "Put on my glasses." Taking a pair of glasses off the desk, he walks back to the window for another look. The scene at first appears the same, but then he sees things he never saw before: "a quiet act of kindness in the shadows, a courageous sacrifice for the sake of justice, a hidden potential in a human soul, a loving embrace in a humble place. And suddenly he feels a great compassion for this lost and lonely humanity. The voice behind him says quietly, 'Until you see what I can see, you cannot feel what I can feel.'"[9]

The dead man's experience in Heaven parallels mine on earth. As a little child, I found my little section of the planet a wondrous place filled with "blue waters, green forests, and white clouds." I uncritically accepted it. I didn't know enough to appreciate it—its beauty was a given. I knew nothing else.

As a young adult, I lost sight of the beauty. My senses were once again overwhelmed, but this time by the horrors of "human selfishness and greed, the ravages of war, and . . . unbridled exploitation." Even now I have to avoid newspapers and evening news if I don't want to be depressed.

But God has taught me to look at things through His glasses. With them on, I not only discover inspiring instances of human compassion but more often feel my own heart going out, like His. It's true—

> The mind has a thousand eyes,
>   And the heart but one;
> Yet the light of a whole life dies
>   When love is done. [10]

The more love is given leave to flourish, the more brightly life's light burns.

It is that light that shines in Henry James's advice to his nephew. The young man asked the great novelist what he ought to do with his life, "how he ought to live it."

"Three things in human life are important," his uncle counseled. "The first is to be kind. The second is to be kind. And the third is to be kind."[11] Kind is what love is; kindness is what love does. Without it the widow's son goes to his grave.

## Jesus Cares Without Regard for Position

Who is this woman that Jesus should feel compassion for her? Luke doesn't tell us, but she probably was nobody. Just "a widow," a nameless face in the crowd. Jesus' lack of concern for people's position or social prestige is so typical we take it for granted. There is nothing of the social climber in Him; He's not politically ambitious. He gains nothing by giving her back her son. She can't do a thing for Him.

Jesus' concern for all people, even those on the lowest rungs of society, impresses me all the more right now because, as I am writing, I am also reading the third volume of Robert Caro's biography of Lyndon Johnson. I gave myself this assignment, not because I'm a Johnson fan, but because he was such a huge presence on the political scene during the years that my political awareness was forming. My curiosity about that era and the men and women who shaped it is insatiable. During that period, Johnson was, according to Caro, the most effective Senate majority leader in history. He was also, by all accounts, a master politician. Unfortunately, in this case I haven't paid him a compliment. Johnson was manipulative, conniving, dishonest, rude, demanding and in every way at all times self-serving, at least during the years covered by this biography. He could also be charming, submissive, courteous, and deferential—when it served his purposes. He quickly amassed enormous power in the Senate by ingratiating himself to the Senate's most influential member, Richard Russell of Georgia. He also ran errands and in other ways made himself indispensable to other members whose favors he was seeking. He did whatever it took to get what he wanted. In the meantime, to his staff and others he considered beneath him, he was ruthless.[12]

The contrast between this ambitious self-server and Jesus could not be greater, at least as Caro tells his story. Unfortunately, Johnson was not unique. Equally unfortunately, Jesus was nearly so.

But not totally. History offers inspiring examples of men and women whose lives Jesus transformed, who followed His example in giving themselves to others without regard for their positions. The most famous of these, undoubtedly, is St. Francis of Assisi. G. K. Chesterton's description of his compassion bears quoting here. If you didn't know better, you'd think he was describing Jesus:

> To him a man stays always a man and does not disappear in a dense crowd any more than in a desert. He honored all men; that is, he not only loved but respected them all. What gave him extraordinary personal power was this: that from the Pope to the beggar, from the sultan of Syria in his pavilion to the ragged robbers crawling out of the wood, there was never a man who looked into those brown burning eyes without being certain that Francis Bernardone was really interested in *him*, in his own inner individual life from the cradle to the grave; that he himself was being valued and taken seriously and not merely added to the spoil of some social policy or the names of some clerical document. . . . He treated the whole mob of men as a mob of kings.[13]

Thus Jesus looked on an unknown woman, who could give nothing in return for the favor He was doing her, without a thought of what He might gain from her. His was not a discriminating, calculating compassion, but love that flowed from His character with a purity that we admire and, in our best moments, seek to imitate.

## Jesus Cares Without a Showy Display of Power

Something else I might have overlooked if I hadn't been studying the life of Lyndon Johnson is that Jesus, in a way so

58

uncharacteristic of the publicity-hungry Johnson, *quietly* called the widow's son back to life. After reassuring her, "he went up and touched the coffin, and those carrying it stood still. He said, 'Young man, I say to you, get up!' The dead man sat up and began to talk, and Jesus gave him back to his mother" (Luke 7:14, 15). That's it. Luke's straightforward account reflects Jesus' matter-of-fact manner, one that will often be repeated countless times later as He intervenes on behalf of the hurting. There's no fanfare, no razzle-dazzle. None of the showmanship so typical of certain religious entertainers who mesmerize their audiences with audacious feats of healing and "supernatural" activity. Johnson, by all accounts, was an audacious performer in the Senate, his deeds only outpaced by his self-promotion. He exercised great power; he "displayed" even more. Jesus didn't.

A very different kind of politician heightens our appreciation of Jesus' manner here. Harry Truman was in the White House as Johnson was rising in the Senate. The president provided the perfect foil for Johnson. In his grasping for ever more clout, Johnson trampled over people's feelings and careers with little regard for the consequences. Truman, on the other hand, never lost awareness of the potential evil, as well as the good, inherent in his high office. Years after he left office in 1953, the retired president observed in a conversation with journalist Eric Sevareid, "What you don't understand is the power of a President to hurt." He added, "that a word, a harsh glance, a peremptory motion by a President of the United States, could so injure another man's pride that it would remain a scar on his emotional system all his life."

Even after he left office, Truman was cautious. He recalled for Sevareid an episode that occurred two years earlier in the late winter or spring of 1962. Following Truman's lecture at a university in southern California, a student asked during the question-and-answer period, "Mr. President, what do you think of our local yokel?" He meant Pat Brown, then governor of California.

Truman, who held the presidency in highest esteem, scolded the boy. He should be ashamed of himself for speaking of the governor of a state so disrespectfully, even if he disagreed with him. The boy, close to tears, sat down.

Immediately after the question period, Truman sought out the boy to explain that he meant nothing personal, that he was dealing with the principle involved. They shook hands. Still not letting the matter rest, the former president later asked the dean to send him reports on the boy's progress in school. The dean said he would, and he did. Truman had the satisfaction of hearing from the young man a few times. "He's doing very well," he told Sevareid.

Sevareid said of the incident, "The simple point here is that Mr. Truman had instantly realized how a public scolding by a former President could mark and mar the boy's inner life and his standing in the community."

I am retelling the story here to get to a comment Sevareid had earlier written about the president. "A man's character is his fate, said the ancient Greeks. Chance, in good part, took Harry Truman to the presidency, but it was his character that kept him there and determined his historical fate. He is, without any doubt, destined to live in the books as one of the strongest and most decisive of the American Presidents."[14]

I was still a boy when Harry Truman left office. His popular standing, according to opinion polls, was at rock bottom. In 1951, he had fired General Douglas MacArthur, who was far more popular than the feisty man in the White House. For a while, some government leaders seriously feared a popular uprising against the president. As a youngster, I never guessed I would live long enough to see Mr. Truman's reputation rise as it has. Historians now regularly place him among the greatest of our presidents. The more they learn about him, the better they like him.

Jesus affects us the same way, doesn't He?

## Jesus Cares Without an Investigation into Their Past

Just as Jesus showed no concern about the widow's social standing, He also asked no questions about her or her son's moral record. No investigation here as to whether the widow and her son were worthy of this great miracle.

This isn't an idle comment. In Jesus' day, sickness was usually attributed to sin. Remember Jesus' healing of the blind man in John 9? "Who sinned, this man or his parents?" they asked Jesus. Like some religious types today, they assumed that a pure life led to a healthy life and a sinful life led to sickness and death.

Jesus didn't ask. He just acted. He demonstrates the same nonjudgmental compassion here that He attributes to God in the Parable of the Prodigal Son in Luke 15. After squandering his inheritance on wine, women, and partying, the foolish young man slides down the slopes of degradation until, in disgrace, he "comes to himself" and goes home, not knowing whether his father will even let him come back. You know the wonderful story. The father, so far from disowning, embraces and restores him. He does not demand a confession of his sins, doesn't ask for repayment of the wasted money, doesn't lay out a program of reform. Instead, he rejoices that his son has come home.

As Jesus rejoices that the widow's son is now fully restored to his mother. His heart went out to her, and He acted. It took "guts" to do that.

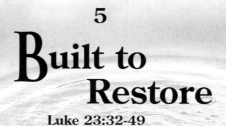

# 5
# Built to Restore

**Luke 23:32-49**

{ "Father, forgive them, for they do not know what they are doing" (Luke 23:34). }

Origen, a third-century church father, asserts in one of his sermons that there are six ways in which a man may gain forgiveness of his sins:

1. by baptism

2. by martyrdom

3. by almsgiving (Luke 11:41)

4. by forgiving others (Matthew 6:14)

5. by love (Luke 7:4, 5)

6. by converting a sinner from his evil ways (James 5:20)[15]

Study his list carefully. If Origen is right and these are the only means of gaining forgiveness, then what are we to do with the thief on the cross? "I tell you the truth, today you will be with me in paradise," Jesus promises him, even though the man has already confessed that he deserves to die. What does Origen think happened to him? The man hasn't been baptized, isn't a martyr, isn't giving money to the poor, says nothing about forgiving anybody else, has no opportunity to demonstrate his love (as did the centurion in Luke 7), and certainly hasn't converted a sinner from his evil ways (unless self-conversion counts). What has he done to earn his forgiveness?

Nothing. And that's the glory of the gospel story. It is also the reason that this thief enters into so many debates on what a person must do to be saved. Jesus promises him salvation even though he has done nothing to earn it. Is he the grand exception to the rule, or are we to understand that Jesus can save whomever He wishes, that the whole point of Jesus' death is to make forgiveness available even to those who can't earn it, which is just about all of us, isn't it?

You can't study the character of Jesus without concluding that a secret of His greatness is mercy. Grace is at the core of the gospel; it is also in the heart of the Savior. Origen's list is not irrelevant, however. We can't dismiss these six items because of Jesus' mercy toward the thief. Though we can't earn salvation, we can—and want to—do what is pleasing to Him in response.

Further, Jesus insists that grace must be in the heart of His disciples. In Luke 7, Jesus has an amazing conversation with Simon the Pharisee. The Pharisees, the strictest of the Jewish sects, were admired for their piety, but no one could accuse them of being soft on sinners. Simon must have been horrified when a woman barged into his home and began lavishing her attention on Jesus. And not just any woman. This one had a past.

> Now one of the Pharisees invited Jesus to have dinner with him, so he went to the Pharisee's house and reclined at the table. When a woman who had lived a sinful life in that town learned that Jesus was eating at the Pharisee's house, she brought an alabaster jar of perfume, and as she stood behind him at his feet weeping, she began to wet his feet with her tears.

Then she wiped them with her hair, kissed them and poured perfume on them.

When the Pharisee who had invited him saw this, he said to himself, "If this man were a prophet, he would know who is touching him and what kind of woman she is—that she is a sinner."

Jesus answered him, "Simon, I have something to tell you."

"Tell me, teacher," he said.

"Two men owed money to a certain moneylender. One owed him five hundred denarii, and the other fifty. Neither of them had the money to pay him back, so he canceled the debts of both. Now which of them will love him more?"

Simon replied, "I suppose the one who had the bigger debt canceled."

"You have judged correctly," Jesus said.

Then he turned toward the woman and said to Simon, "Do you see this woman? I came into your house. You did not give me any water for my feet, but she wet my feet with her tears and wiped them with her hair. You did not give me a kiss, but this woman, from the time I entered, has not stopped kissing my feet. You did not put oil on my head, but she has poured perfume on my feet. Therefore, I tell you, her many sins have been forgiven—for she loved much. But he who has been forgiven little loves little."

Then Jesus said to her, "Your sins are forgiven."

The other guests began to say among themselves, "Who is this who even forgives sins?"

{ Jesus said to the woman, "Your faith has saved you;
go in peace" (Luke 7:36-50).

If we had been a guest at that dinner, we also would have been shocked, don't you think? In the first place, the woman's behavior was most unseemly. And from the Pharisees' perspective, so was Jesus'. No self-respecting Pharisee would have allowed this woman of ill repute to come near him, let alone to kiss and anoint him. Even more offensive was Jesus' offer of forgiveness. He was not unaware of her sordid reputation, yet didn't require any acts of penitence. With a word, He set her free from her past. Simon was naturally offended at Jesus' presumption. (Where did Jesus get His authority to forgive sins?)

Instead of defending himself, Jesus taught His host an unforgettable lesson on forgiveness. It's a lesson He returned to repeatedly and the one that crowned His ministry when, on the cross, He forgives the thief next to Him. In light of all His previous teaching, we shouldn't be surprised. We shouldn't be, but we can't help wondering . . .

## How Could He Do It?
## How Could He Forgive His Own Assassins?

It's one thing to turn the other cheek, as He has taught us to do, but quite another to forgive people in the very act of taking your life. To get even would be a whole lot more satisfying. Alexander Pope said it so well: "To err is human, to forgive divine." People in any kind of public leadership role are never free of critics and ill-wishers. Oh, how good it would feel to pay them back! To refuse to retaliate requires a maturity most of us just don't have.

Among prominent Americans, Abraham Lincoln seems to come the closest to Jesus in his mercy for enemies. His graciousness toward the South, his determination to bring the rebels back into the Union without recrimination, and his quickness to pardon offenses were not understood by—indeed, were not acceptable to—most politicians and leaders in the North. A letter he received from the businessmen on the Chicago Board of Trade spoke for the majority. The president and secretary of the board wrote the letter, reciting the terrible evils Union prisoners suffered in the overcrowded Confederate prison camp at Andersonville, Georgia. There the men, quartered in an open field without tents or huts, were exposed to the elements, without adequate clothes and food, dying of disease, all but totally neglected.

It was only just, the Chicago leaders argued, for the federal government to set aside an equal number of Confederate prisoners in northern camps and subject them to the same treatment: "Throw them in together in such a way that most of them would die and the rest would lose their health and their minds, do it deliberately and with calculation, in order that there might be a fair extension of pain and death."

"We are aware," wrote the Chicagoans, "that this, our petition, savors of cruelty"—but it was no time to be squeamish. There was a war on and they felt obliged to "urge retaliatory measures as a matter of necessity."[16]

An eye for an eye, they wanted, a tooth for a tooth.

It was only fair. They did it to our side; we must do it to theirs. This same reasoning always drives nations (including ours) to war and perpetuates the worst kinds of barbarity. All we want is what is fair.

Lincoln wanted something else, something more. He wanted what would restore, not destroy, the enemy. Vengeance was far from the heart of the president. Historians still ponder what it would have been like if Lincoln had lived to preside over the post-war recovery. His unshakable determination to hold the union together would have been followed by his loving insistence that the rebels be forgiven and restored to full citizenship. How different subsequent American history would have been if grace had prevailed.

Lincoln learned about grace the same place we do, in the life and death of Jesus. On the cross He taught us that genuine forgiveness knows no limits.

## He Could Forgive . . .

### Because He Had Made an Earlier Commitment

On the cross He prayed, "Father, into your hands I commit my spirit," but this was nothing new for Jesus. Years earlier He had placed himself in the Father's hands. That's what He was talking about as a youth in the temple (see Luke 2). That certainly was what He was demonstrating at His baptism (see Luke 3). He was on earth to do His Father's will. If that will included suffering the betrayal and denial of His disciples and enduring false accusations and undeserved conviction and execution, so be it. What He would not do is run from God's will or turn on the people He had come to serve. His purpose was to save, not to condemn. He would be faithful to His mission.

The apostle Paul later expressed this same commitment in an unforgettable passage in his letter to the Philippians. Writing in prison, his fate uncertain, Paul reassured his friends in Philippi that he was not worried about his fate. Whether he lived or died was immaterial to him. What mattered was that either dead or alive, he should do his best for Christ:

> Yes, and I will continue to rejoice, for I know that
> through your prayers and the help given by the
> Spirit of Jesus Christ, what has happened to me
> will turn out for my deliverance. I eagerly expect
> and hope that I will in no way be ashamed, but
> will have sufficient courage so that now as always
> Christ will be exalted in my body, whether by life
> or by death. For to me, to live is Christ and to die
> is gain. If I am to go on living in the body, this will
> mean fruitful labor for me. Yet what shall I choose?
> I do not know! I am torn between the two: I desire
> to depart and be with Christ, which is better by
> far; but it is more necessary for you that I remain
> in the body. Convinced of this, I know that I will
> remain, and I will continue with all of you for your
> progress and joy in the faith, so that through my
> being with you again your joy in Christ Jesus will
> overflow on account of me (Philippians 1:18-26).

He could face his future with serenity because he had placed his life in the Lord's hands. So had Jesus.

## Because He Believed They Didn't Know What They Were Doing

"Father, forgive them, for they do not know what they are doing" (Luke 23:34). Like mobs everywhere, the many are pawns in the hands of the few; these have been whipped into a frenzy by Jesus' enemies. There was so much they didn't know.

"Forgive them," *because they don't really know me.* They can't see that Jesus is really on their side. His whole purpose for being has been to live—and now to die—for them. If they only understood . . .

They aren't the only ones. People still don't know Jesus and because they don't, they fear and reject Him. The grace He offers they cannot, or will not, accept.

Arthur Miller relates a touching story of Marilyn Monroe's unfortunate introduction to Jesus. Her experience has been duplicated, one way or another, by all too many others. When she was only 5 or 6 years old, the fundamentalist church to which her foster family belonged held a huge open-air service. As part of the pageantry, "hundreds of children, all dressed alike, the girls in white dresses and the boys in blue trousers and white shirts, stood ranged against the sides of a tremendous natural amphitheatre somewhere in the mountains in the Los Angeles area. Each girl had a cape, red on one side and white on the other, and at the start they wore the red side out. On signal during a revivalist hymn they were all to turn their capes inside out, from sinful red to the pure white of the saved. Magically the mountainside turned white on the proper verse of the hymn."

Almost all the mountainside, that is. There was one red dot in the middle. Telling the story as an adult, Miss Monroe would laugh like the little girl she once was and explain that she just "clean forgot." She was so interested in the sight and so proud of the children for remembering to turn their capes inside out on cue that she forgot she was supposed to do it also. She was still relating her story 25 years later, always laughing about it.

It was funny to the adult, but the little girl was beaten for messing up the show. They told her Jesus condemned her also. She was led to believe it was only one instance of God's "irremediable" dislike. "Jesus is supposed to be so forgiving, but they never mentioned that; he was basically out to smack you in the head if you did something wrong."[17]

So a little girl was turned away from Jesus. If the adults had really known Jesus, they'd have "suffer[ed] the little [one] to come unto" Him:

> Jesus said to his disciples: "Things that cause
> people to sin are bound to come, but woe to that
> person through whom they come. It would be
> better for him to be thrown into the sea with a
> millstone tied around his neck than for him to
> cause one of these little ones to sin (Luke 17:1, 2).

## Because They Didn't Know Themselves

Of all of them, the criminals and crowd, only one voice—the thief's—speaks with insight:

> "Don't you fear God," he said [to the other convict],
> "since you are under the same sentence? We are
> punished justly, for we are getting what our deeds
> deserve. But this man has done nothing wrong."
>
> Then he said, "Jesus, remember me when you
> come into your kingdom" (Luke 23:40-42).

In the Gospels, sinners often show a clearer self-insight than the so-called righteous. The murderous crowd can rush to judgment only by denying their own culpability. The thief stands out because he alone admits his guilt. He doesn't try to prove he's as good as the next fellow. He knows better. As a result, there's hope for him.

Karl Barth, one of the twentieth century's leading theologians, is as remarkable for his grasp of his own need for God's grace as for his towering intelligence and outpouring of theological tomes. Once, when talking with Hans Kung, another famed theologian, he confessed his dependence:

> When once the day comes when I have to appear
> before my Lord, then I will not come with my
> deeds, with the volumes of my *Dogmatics* in the
> basket upon my back. All the angels there would
> have to laugh. But then I shall also not say, "I have

{ always meant well; I had good faith." No, then I will only say one thing: "Lord, be merciful to me a poor sinner!"[18]

What else can an honest person say?

### Because They Didn't Know God's Will

They sneered, "He saved others; let him save himself if he is the Christ of God, the Chosen One." They mocked, "If you are the king of the Jews, save yourself." They read the notice above him, "This is the King of the Jews." They asked, "Aren't you the Christ? Save yourself and us!"

They knew the titles. They just didn't grasp what they meant. They believed in God, but they didn't catch on to what He was doing. They just thought they did.

### Because They Couldn't Foresee the Consequences

They don't know they are caught up in something far, far greater than themselves. They have no idea that in ridding themselves of this troublesome teacher, they are playing into God's hands, participating in the most consequential death of all time, and paving the way for a miraculous resurrection that will change the course of all subsequent history. The words their ancient forbear Joseph spoke to his brothers could be spoken to them as well: "You intended to harm me, but *God intended it for good to accomplish what is now being done, the saving of many lives*" (Genesis 50:20, italics mine).

### Because It's About Relationships

Jesus didn't worry about vindicating himself, proving His innocence, or getting even with His tormentors, because He had something far more important on His mind: "the saving of many lives." He came to restore people to their proper relationship with God. He came to heal broken hearts and broken homes. He is still doing so.

In my files is a letter from a heartbroken father. He writes that his daughter and son-in-law are so angry with him over an earlier disagreement that they will have little to do with him or his wife. The daughter has token contact with them, but the son-in-law will not speak to them; he has rebuffed every effort at reconciliation. The father admits he said some harsh things in the heat of a disagreement, but he later apologized (and apologized), but to no avail. He has not been forgiven.

His letter is a confessional as well as an apology. At the time he wrote the letter, he had a growing leadership role in his church. He brought up an earlier sin for which he had repented and been forgiven. That was in the past, but he mentioned it again because he didn't want to hurt the church and was prepared to step out of any further role if I felt he should. He also valued our friendship and didn't want it to be affected. Here's part of my answer to him:

> You want to know what this will do to our relationship. This is an easy one. Nothing. No one who has lived as long as I have has any right to condemn his brother. From time to time people tell me their sins and I can rather smugly rejoice because theirs aren't mine. But I can't rejoice long, since I have had my own struggles and, like the publican in Jesus' story, dare not lift my eyes godward and certainly have no righteousness to proclaim.
>
> Next you ask where you go from here. You go right ahead making your plans, doing your preparing, and seeking His will in serving Him. If He only let the completely pure ones among us serve Him, His ranks would be very, very thin.
>
> As I read His word, I note that many whom He called to serve Him were flawed, some terribly so.

How would you like to have on your conscience the shortcomings of David or Solomon or Peter or Paul? I mention them specifically because they've given me hope. If God can use them, there's room for me, too, maybe.

I wish it were otherwise, but I seriously wonder whether we genuinely learn compassion except by our own need of it. When I was a young man, my spirit of judgment was harsh, just as harsh as my untried confidence allowed. Now that I am older, and tried, and far less than the perfect person I wanted—and want—to be, I realize I have no right to utter a syllable against another, and certainly no right to spurn an apology.

The sad end of this story is that a couple of years ago, the son-in-law—no longer young, having left his wife and children and made a disaster of his professional life—committed suicide. He had alienated himself from just about everybody. He would not be reconciled. Eventually, alone and bitter, he ended it all.  His father- and mother-in-law, on the other hand, now enjoy a close relationship with their daughter and grand-children. Their mutual forgiveness led to a beautiful and lasting reconciliation.

If it's a relationship you want, you must be prepared to forgive. And forgive. And forgive.

For if you forgive men when they sin against you, your heavenly Father will also forgive you. But if you do not forgive men their sins, your Father will not forgive your sins (Matthew 6:14, 15).

And when you stand praying, if you hold anything against anyone, forgive him, so that your Father in heaven may forgive you your sins (Mark 11:25).

# 6

# Built to Relate

## Luke 8:1-3

> After this, Jesus traveled about . . .
> proclaiming the good news of the
> kingdom of God. The Twelve were with
> him, and also some women. . . . These
> women were helping to support them
> out of their own means
> (Luke 8:1-3).

As we have already seen, character cannot be separated from relationships. Basically, *character* is the word for how we relate to and treat other people. That's *all* other people, regardless of their rank, religion, race—or their gender.

Most studies of Jesus' relationships concentrate on the call, training, and empowering of the 12, His closest disciples. Not until recent years has much attention been paid to the women in His company with the predictable exception of Mother's Day sermons. Perhaps because most of us preachers are male, we feel more comfortable talking about how men deal with one another. We really don't understand women (as our wives regularly remind us). In this chapter, though, I'm going to venture out, but not very far—only far enough to point out a few things men and women have in common. It's not a chapter about women—I wouldn't presume—but about the essence of relationships.

Reading Luke 8:1-3 reminds me of the women who have blessed my life. My wife of 44 years heads the list, of course. I can't imagine life without her. There have been many others as well—my grandmothers, mother, sister, daughters, cousins, aunts, nieces, granddaughters (and adoptive great-granddaughter), work assistants and associates, and female friends. To have lived in an all-male world without these deep, often complex, sometimes perplexing but always enriching relationships would have deprived me of some of life's greatest satisfactions. Beyond a doubt all of us, male and female, need both of us, male and female.

Luke gets specific. These are not just "the ladies, bless their hearts" to Luke. They are individuals with something in common: Jesus has healed them. Only one instance is singled out though. Jesus drove Mary Magdalene's seven demons away. Luke doesn't tell us what He did for the others. He mentions Joanna, Cuza's wife; Luke doesn't describe her affliction, but he wants us to know she's a woman of substance. Her husband holds a high administrative post in Herod's household. Luke's early readers probably would have known or known of Susanna, so he just mentions her name. There were, in addition, "many others."

This brief passage gives us a clue to relationship building, one often overlooked by people who "just want to be friends" but can never seem to pull it off. Friendship is reciprocal. It's both give and take. Jesus healed these women. In return, they "were helping to support" Jesus and His disciples out of their own means. They had received, so they gave.

Before they gave support, they gave thanks. Friendship is also dependent on gratitude. We have already seen that without forgiveness, you can't sustain a long-term relationship. Without gratitude, you can scarcely begin one.

In this chapter, we'll focus on these two elements plus one other. We'll begin with gratitude.

## Gratitude—Seeking Ways to Say Thanks

Think for a moment of the importance of giving thanks within the family. When children are small, parents do most of the giving. A baby is all take and no give. Helpless, dependent, unable to do even the simplest things without assistance, a baby requires constant care. Follow the baby up through the toddler stage. Without adult assistance, will she walk? Will she talk? Will she survive? Move on up to the school years, when Mom becomes the taxi driver, the cheerleader, the healer of bumps and scratches and bruised egos, and Dad works harder than ever to earn the money to pay for the ever-increasing costs this child incurs. I realize that in the modern home, probably both Mom and Dad are working and the roles get all tangled up. The constant, though, is that the parents are the ones doing most of the giving.

It's to be expected, but not to be taken for granted. Children who do not learn to say thanks usually end up as bitter, lonely adults. They cannot keep a marriage or even a friendship together. They expect to be taken care of by others in the family, by other people, by the government, by the world—but give little in return.

Lately, we've noticed a subtle shift in our family. The children (our offspring and our "adoptive" kids) are no longer young. They are settled men and women with families and responsibilities of their own. There isn't much we can do for them anymore. Instead, they now ask what they can do for us. After Joy and I embarked on our year-long motor home tour of North America, we were reluctant to tell them if anything went wrong because (1) they would worry and (2) they would drop whatever they were doing to bail us out of trouble. This took some discipline on our part, by the way, because all kinds of things went wrong. We didn't confess the problems until later, after we had muddled through, lest they should drop everything and come across the country to take care of us. It was enough for us to know that they would be there for us if we really needed them.

Why would they do that? Because they are grateful. They haven't taken for granted our help in their earlier, more dependent years. Thanks to their concern, Joy and I don't worry about our old age. Unlike Shakespeare's King Lear, who grumbled that "sharper than a serpent's tooth" it was to have an ungrateful child, we thank God that our children learned gratitude.

We have been spared the hurt we read about in one of Dear Abby's columns. She said she had run it several times. It resonated apparently with many families who pressed her to republish it.

Before high school commencement, she reports, a proud father took his son, as was common in their well-to-do neighborhood, to pick out a new car as his graduation gift. After searching for a long time, "Bill" selected the car of his dreams.

On the day before graduation, instead of giving him keys to the new car, as Bill had anticipated, his father gave him a Bible that had been carefully wrapped. Bill didn't even open it. He slammed it down and angrily left the house.

He didn't come back that night. In fact he didn't come back until after his father's death. Then he returned and began going through his father's things. In so doing he found the Bible and opened it. Inside he found a check that his father had put there for him. It was made out for the amount needed to buy the car he had longed for. "Sharper than a serpent's tooth . . ."

Back in the high-rolling 1980s, when America was rocked again and again by the exposure of corruption in high places, Ivan Boesky, successful arbitrageur who was often the target of investigations, famously told some business school students, "Greed is all right, by the way. I want you to know that I think greed is healthy. You can be greedy and still feel good about yourself."[19] Satisfying one's greed is obviously a high priority for many Americans. Boesky is right—if what is most important is feeling good about yourself and if your opinion is the only one that matters, grab for all you can get. You'll be able to entertain yourself in your old age, then, like Disney's Scrooge McDuck, rollick in your gold coins. But you'll rollick alone. Like Dear Abby's "Bill," if you don't get what you're grasping for, you'll stomp out—out of the house, out of any relationship. Stomp out often enough and there'll be nobody left to get away from.

This "gimme" attitude is delightfully (though sadly) captured in a perennial campaign story that has been variously attributed to Senators Lyndon Johnson, Emanuel Celler, and Alben Barkeley, among others. When I first heard it, it was attributed to Winston Churchill. This is Speaker of the House Sam Rayburn's version. It seems a freshman representative received a letter from one of his staunchest supporters letting him know he was going to oppose him for reelection. Extremely upset, the congressman hurried home to discuss the matter in person.

"Isn't it true," he asked his constituent, "that not too long ago I helped you get your son out of jail?"

"Yes," admitted the man.

"And isn't it true," the congressman went on, "that I helped you get a scholarship for your daughter?"

"Yes," said the man.

"Then why, why are you opposing me in the coming election?"

The man looked hurt. "But congressman," he exclaimed, "what have you done for me *lately*?"[20]

On the other hand, as I write, names and faces are surfacing of quiet people whom you would not know but who have blessed Joy and me and our family beyond our deserving because once, now a long time ago, their pastor was able to do a little something for them. They have never stopped feeling and expressing their thankfulness. Do I need to tell you that these are healthy people, loved and loving, surrounded by friends and family who adore them?

They are grateful to God as well. That gratitude dominates their worship and binds them to the church. Os Guinness gives examples of some such people whose names you might know:

> The great Czech composer Antonin Dvorak began writing his new music with the words, "with God" and ended "God be thanked." Bach: [wrote] in the margins of his music "SDG" (*Soli Deo Gloria*) and "Glory to the Lamb." Augustine described the Christian as an "alleluia from head to foot." George Herbert, a seventeenth-century Anglican poet, wrote a prayer in one of his poems, "You have given so much to me. Give me one thing more—a grateful heart." G. K. Chesterton stated as "the chief idea of my life" the practice of "taking things with gratitude and not taking things for granted." [The poet] W. H. Auden, "Let your last thinks be all thanks."
>
> Dostoevsky was so aware of the deep importance of gratitude in his own life that he was troubled for humankind if God were not there to be thanked: "Who is man going to love then?" he asks in

{ *The Brothers Karamazov.* "To whom will he be thankful? To whom will he sing his hymn?"[21]

Luke doesn't state that the women are helping Jesus out of their own means because of their gratitude. He just lets us know that first Jesus healed them, and then they supported Him. What else, though, could be their motivation?

## Reciprocity—It Takes Two to Seal the Deal

If gratitude is the motive, reciprocity is the result. Jesus helped these women when they were hurting; now it's their turn to do something for Him and they are gladly acting out their gratitude.

Something else needs to be underscored, which is for me (and I suspect for you) the hard part: He accepts their help. Do you find it strange that He whose Father owns the cattle on a thousand hills receives donations from these persons of relatively modest means? Are you like me in finding it difficult to accept gifts from people you have helped?

I have a rather prickly friend who finds it almost impossible to receive. He gives generously; he receives begrudgingly, sometimes almost insultingly. He could be accused of being a control freak, I suppose. Perhaps that's why he won't let me pay him back for any favors he's done. I can't reciprocate. I know I need work on becoming a more giving person; he doesn't know it, but he is teaching me to become a more "receiving" one.

The Greek philosopher Aristotle believed so strongly in the importance of friendship—and understood so well how difficult its maintenance can be—that he devoted more than a fifth of his classic book *Nicomachean Ethics* to the subject. He didn't consider anyone happy who did not enjoy a thriving friend-ship. He wrote more than three centuries before Christ, yet his insights are still helpful. He believed there were three categories of friendships:

1. *Mutual-interest friendships.* These make up a large part of our lives and include such people as those in your reading group, members of your country club, your colleagues, car pool associates, fellow church members, and the like.

2. *Mutual-pleasure friendships.* These are among people you enjoy hanging out with. You shop, fish, party, visit galleries, bowl, work, and play with them. This is the most popular category and is usually what we mean when we speak of our friends.

3. *Mutual-values friendships.* These are persons who share your basic beliefs, your ethics, your sensitivities. They constitute, Aristotle believed, your truest friendships.[22]

Three categories but one constant: "mutual." It takes two: sharing interests, sharing pleasures, holding similar values.

Edgar A. Guest, whose genius could often dilute profound truths into light verse, expresses both the gratitude and give-and-take of lasting relationships in this well-circulated Christmas poem:

> I'd like to be the sort of friend that you have
> been to me;
> > I'd like to be the help that you've been always
> > glad to be;
> I'd like to mean as much to you each minute of
> the day
> > As you have meant, old friend of mine, to me
> > along the way.

I'd like to do the big things and the splendid things
for you,
> To brush the gray from out your skies and leave
> them only blue;
I'd like to say the kindly things that I so oft have
heard,
> And feel that I could rouse your soul the way
> that mine you've stirred.

I'd like to give you back the joy that you have
given me,
> Yet that were wishing you a need I hope will
> never be;
I'd like to make you feel as rich as I, who travel on
> Undaunted in the darkest hours with you to
> lean upon.

I'm wishing at this Christmas time that I could
but repay
> A portion of the gladness that you've strewn
> along my way;
And could I have one wish this year, this only
would it be:
> I'd like to be the sort of friend that you have
> been to me.[23]

Gratitude and reciprocity meet in many New Testament instructions on the proper way for Christians to treat one another. Christ has given us so much; no matter how thankful we feel, we can't return as much as we have received from Him. What we can do, however, is pass the favor on. We can say thanks to Christ in our love for and good treatment of others:

> A new command I give you: Love one another. As
> I have loved you, so you must love one another. By
> this all men will know that you are my disciples, if
> you love one another (John 13:34, 35).

{ Be devoted to one another in brotherly love. Honor one another above yourselves (Romans 12:10).

{ Be completely humble and gentle; be patient, bearing with one another in love (Ephesians 4:2).

{ Be kind and compassionate to one another, forgiving each other, just as in Christ God forgave you (Ephesians 4:32).

## Good Grammar—with Specific Attention to Pronouns

A third element needs some attention here. It's not mentioned in Luke 8, but it is a requirement of genuinely grateful, reciprocal relationships. Pardon me for sounding like the English teacher I used to be. It's been many years since I tried to teach the uses of language to high school and college students. Grammar was not their most exciting subject. I usually did not convert them to a love of language. If I could teach those classes again, I'd talk less about the "boring rules" and more about meaningful relationships, because that's what grammar is about.

Relationships are spelled out primarily in prepositions, which tell how a person, place, or thing "relates" to another. It (whatever "it" is) is either in, out, of, over, under, beside, beyond, with, without, along, among, or beside another. (The possibilities, of course, are much greater than this brief list.) The use of prepositions is perhaps the hardest part of learning English as a second language. They are so easy to misunderstand; they so subtly change the meaning of a verb or sentence. Do you talk up, talk down, talk down to, talk about, talk around, talk beside, talk over, talk beyond, talk with . . . ? Prepositions are difficult to get right because proper relationships are difficult to get right.

But when it comes to personal relationships, the key words aren't prepositions but pronouns: me, mine, myself, you, yours, yourself, they, theirs, themselves, and so on. No other words betray the real person more than these personal pronouns. Is it about me or about us? Did I do it or did we? Is it mine or ours? Am I doing this for you or for me? Or for us?

Language, as everybody knows, is our primary instrument of communication. Communication, though, is seldom employed purely for the purpose of transmitting and receiving information. It also functions to express emotion, define relative positions, and close distances or enlarge them. And as has often been pointed out, the most important thing in communication is to hear what isn't being said. But another very important thing is to pay close attention to the pronouns.

Some time ago, I received an advertising brochure from an organization specializing in church growth. Usually I toss junk mail, but this one I read. As a pastor, I have long been a student of how churches grow. This one, though, after catching my attention, quickly went into the wastebasket. The bold letters across the top promised what couldn't be delivered: "Eliminate communication problems forever!" they shouted. "That's false advertising!" I shouted back.

The first paragraph compounded the crime: "Proper communication is a key ingredient to any successful ministry. To ensure healthy communication between you, your members, and your staff you need a detailed policy manual designed specifically for *your* ministry."

More often than not, policy manuals confuse rather than clarify. No manual can "eliminate communication problems forever." It can spell out the administrative hierarchy, detail procedures, and list the rules, but it can't do a thing to correct the misuse of pronouns. Wherever *I* rules, *we* suffers. If it's *mine*, *you* do without. If it's all about *me*, it's never about *us*.

Let me tell you about one man who understood this principle. To someone of my generation growing up during World War II, the peace and unity in modern western Europe is amazing. Traveling through Portugal, France, Switzerland, and Italy, for example, using a common currency (the Euro), and crossing borders without a passport is an experience we never thought possible in earlier years when suspicion, not friendship, was reciprocated among the nations.

Nobody has been more responsible for this era of goodwill than France's Jean Monnet. Quietly, patiently, determinedly, he devoted his life to bringing lasting peace to the war-torn continent. He often quoted his friend Dwight Morrow, "There are two kinds of people in politics: those who want to *be somebody*, and those who want to *do something*." Monnet belonged to the latter group. He did things, and he never sought credit for what he did. It was always about *us*, never about *me*. For 70 years he worked for European unity. I had read about this remarkable man many years ago, but only recently have I learned more of the pivotal role he played in the Lend-Lease program through which America gave desperately needed help to Great Britain early in World War II, and later with the Marshall Plan through which America sent even more desperately needed assistance to a Western Europe digging out from the rubble. According to James Reston, Monnet was also a key figure in the early days of the League of Nations and a financial advisor to China, Austria, and Poland.

What made him so effective, Reston concluded, was that "he lacked all the attributes usually associated with politicians. He was almost invisible in the Allied meetings—a roly-poly, rosy-cheeked little man, bald as a peeled onion. He lived simply in Houjarray outside Paris. . . . He was not a very good public speaker, *but he listened in four languages* [italics mine] and won the trust of all the squabbling Allied leaders because he was precise, informed, and detached, and he never spoke ill of people or tried to displace them."[24]

What a wonderful statement: "He listened in four languages." Most of us find it difficult to listen in one! And that's because, if the conversation isn't about *me*, my mind wanders. Monnet paid attention, though; it was always about *us*.

A comment by Professor Martin Marty of the University of Chicago, in accepting the Skirball Values Award in California a couple years ago, provides keen insight into Monnet's effectiveness—and wraps up the point I'm trying to make about pronouns. "Argument is based on the answer," he said, "conversation on the question. In argument 'I' know the answer and must defeat, convert, or expel you, and vice versa. In conversation, 'we' know the question and must interact, respect, and learn from each other."[25]

You see, we must pay attention to the pronouns.

Thank you for bearing with this old English teacher. As I said, there's nothing specifically about pronouns in Luke 8. I've taken us on this little side trip, though, because for years I've been studying how groups of all kinds work—committees, congregations, families, legislative bodies, and sports teams. In this respect, these women in Jesus' company are symbolic of all groups. Luke doesn't let us listen in on their conversations, but he tells us enough to be certain of their gratitude and desire to give back to the one who saved them. You can count on it. They were watching their pronouns.

For any group to survive, it really must be about *us*.

# 7

# Built to Go Boldly

### Luke 18:31-33

> Jesus took the Twelve aside and told them, ". . . everything that is written by the prophets about the Son of Man will be fulfilled. He will be handed over to the Gentiles. They will mock him, insult him, spit on him, flog him and kill him. On the third day he will rise again" (Luke 18:31-33).

Gregory Peck died last year. Most moviegoers of my generation, if asked to name the five Hollywood personalities they most admired, would quickly mention Peck's name, most likely at the head of the list. He is one actor who seemed to have it all: resonant bass voice ("this is God speaking"), commanding physical presence, masculine good looks, and Oscar-worthy performances. Richard Corliss, in his eulogy of the actor in *Time* magazine writes, "By all accounts, the reel and the real Gregory Peck were close kin. He was a model of probity, a loyal friend to colleagues in distress, a father confessor to the Hollywood community. He chaired the National Society of This, the American Academy of That. He was laden with official honors: Lyndon Johnson gave him the Presidential Medal of Freedom; Richard Nixon put him on his Enemies List."[26]

For many of us, Peck's premier role was not as General Douglas MacArthur or Captain Horatio Hornblower or *Moby Dick's* Captain Ahab, but as the courageous white attorney Atticus Finch in the movie based on Harper Lee's novel, *To Kill a Mockingbird*. In 2002, the American Film Institute voted Atticus Finch the top hero in United States movie history. The drama was set in Alabama in the racist 1930s, when it was unheard of for a white man to defend an African-American (even though innocent) from the charge of raping a white woman. Corliss sums up Finch's performance in court, "He argues his case brilliantly, demolishes the opposition, convinces each member of the movie audience . . . and loses."

In portraying the fearless lawyer who did everything right and still lost his case, Atticus Finch won our hearts. When Peck died, author Harper Lee accorded him the highest possible praise. "Gregory Peck was a beautiful man," she said. "Atticus Finch gave him the opportunity to play himself."

What makes a man beautiful? To everyone who knew him, Peck was a man of character. And character, though it has many facets, must show courage above all or it is not character. No matter how hostile the crowd, how powerful the temptation, how seemingly hopeless the cause, character neither cowers nor retreats.

> The wicked man flees though no one pursues,
> but the righteous are as bold as a lion
> (Proverbs 28:1).

Jesus also had "the opportunity to play himself" and proved to be "a beautiful man." This brief study of His character would be incomplete without a chapter devoted to courage, the kind He displayed throughout His brief life—and the kind He calls us to. The kind that is not the spectacular heroics of swashbuckling films but the quiet, steely resolve that enabled Atticus Finch to stand against the life-threatening prejudice of his community and Jesus to stand against the growing hostility of His powerful, and ultimately successful, enemies.

Courage is too complex a topic for thorough exploration here. Others have done it better. My favorite title on the subject is Paul Tillich's *The Courage to Be* because it implies that living itself requires courage. Because not everyone has it, some never achieve the fullness of life (the "being") that Jesus holds out: "The thief comes only to steal and kill and destroy; I have come that they may have life, and have it to the full" (John 10:10).

We'll take up two aspects suggested by the life of Jesus: the bravery to go where you've never gone before, and the fortitude to go even though you know what you are in for when you get there.

## The Courage to Go Where You've Never Gone Before

Jesus is the inspiration for this section as well as the following, but the language, as every Trekky will recognize, is from the opening words of *Star Trek*: "These are the voyages of the *Starship Enterprise*. Its five-year mission: to explore strange new worlds, to seek out new life and new civilizations, to boldly go where no man has gone before!" No television series stimulated the imaginations of more children (and adults!). Movies were spun off, sequels followed, fan clubs were founded, and books and toys were adopted as emblems for a vast cult of devotees.

Most of the fans probably aren't aware, though, of the echoes of the true story that inspired the series. I wasn't either until I read Tony Horwitz's *Blue Latitudes: Boldly Going Where Captain Cook Has Gone Before.*[27] Among our travels, Joy and I included the American Northwest, Canadian Northeast, Hawaii, and Australia. These are all places the amazing

Captain James Cook explored in the eighteenth century. This intrepid Yorkshire farm boy wrote in his diary that he had sailed "farther than any other man has been before." Captain James Cook took along a naturalist, a surgeon, and "musket-toting, red-jacketed marines." *Star Trek's* Captain James Kirk "beamed down" to planets with his science officer Mr. Spock, his physician Dr. McCoy, and his "phaser-wielding, red-jerseyed 'expendables.'" Both captains were on a course to discover and describe new lands, and both prevailed in spite of the most severe dangers.

Few of us face the challenges of these venturers into the unknown, but life demands that all of us go where at least *we've* never been before. Learning to walk, exploring the backyard, checking out the neighborhood, entering first grade (or preschool or kindergarten), going off to college, enlisting in the military, getting married, having children, changing jobs. . . . Vibrant life consists of breaking through the boundaries of former experience. Dying begins with the retreat from the edges, when fear or inability holds us back.

Even more courage is demanded in relationships. Standing up to bullies, insisting on justice, assisting the downtrodden, defending the embattled—risking your career or your life to save a nobody from certain death.

Jesus' life is a model of this kind of courage. "Who is this man?" was asked of Him time and again. He didn't fit any mold. He came from Nazareth, a nowhere place. As a youngster, He debated the scholars in the temple (see Luke 2). He set out on His own in a ministry of teaching and healing. He had no established headquarters—"Foxes have holes and birds of the air have nests, but the Son of Man has no place to lay his head" (Luke 9:58). He broke social norms to rescue society's rejects. He pressed on in the face of ever-growing animosity. He went where no other prophet had gone before.

Those who would be like Him will press on as well. To sound the retreat is to begin to die.

A delightful cartoon in an astronomy book says it all. Published shortly after astronaut John Glenn's return to space as a daring septuagenarian, the panel shows the determined 77-year-old soaring through space, peering over the spaceship's "steering wheel," and loudly exulting, "To OLDLY go where no man has gone before!" Behind him other spacecraft are honking, and Glenn's backseat drivers are urging him, if they can't orbit faster, to at least move out of the passing lane.[28]

For many of his compatriots, Glenn's return to space was inspiring. He'd been there before, but not like this. Not as an old man. Not as the first man to test whether someone his age could withstand the rigors of space travel. It wasn't just a publicity stunt (although it was undoubtedly that as well), but another piercing of the boundaries, another test of personal bravery.

Senator John Glenn was America's "Golden Boy of the Space Age." He was the first American to orbit the earth. After leaving the space program, he became a distinguished senator from Ohio. Then at 77, he became the oldest person ever to fly in space. Not much scientific information was gained by his excursion, but NASA recaptured the public's imagination. That was about all. Except for one thing: it was one more blow struck on behalf of the aging. We could nudge one another with a wink and a grin and a "You see? He still has it. And so do I! We aren't just grave fodder. Not yet. Not by a long shot!"

I know, I know. My age is showing again. It has crept onto too many pages of this book. But authors write out of their own experience, and mine is that of a man newly retired. For the second time.

My first retirement was in 1999, when I left the pastorate of Central Christian Church in Mesa, Arizona, after 20 years as senior minister. The church sent me off in a blaze of glory (or, more precisely, to the roar of the Harley-Davidson® they gave me as a retirement gift). Now we're into our second retirement. In 2003, I stepped down as president of Hope International University in Fullerton, California, after a 13-year tenure (nine of them shared with Central Christian). Since then Joy and I have been going where we've never gone before—touring North America in a motor home. We are "oldly" going, but we are really fulfilling an old dream.

In my early forties, I began proposing to Joy that, when the children were raised and gone, I should quit my job and we should sell the house, buy a motor home, and travel until we had spent the equity. Then I'd go back to work again. For 25 years it was all talk because when our last child left home, our church was in a building program and I couldn't leave. We stayed in the building program for nearly 20 years. So we waited until my second retirement.

And now we are doing it. I'm writing this chapter in Maryland, on the other edge of the continent from our former California home. We sold the house, bought the motor home, sold the car, and bought a pickup truck to pull behind the motor home. (We had to have the pickup to haul the Harley. You can't leave it home when you don't have a home.) It would have helped if I possessed a whole lot more mechanical savvy than I do. Even a little bit would help. More than once, when faced with yet another mechanical breakdown or, as I'll explain later, a serious accident, I wondered whether we were right "to oldly go."

But this chapter is about courage. Even as a youngster I learned that if I went only where I wasn't afraid to go, I wouldn't go very far. And if I did only what wouldn't get me in trouble, I couldn't do very much. So young or oldly . . . go.

## Go Even Though You Know What You're in for When You Get There

The first facet of courage is far more common than the second. All of us have to go where we've never been before, especially in our younger years. We could not have reached adulthood otherwise.

But as adults, our steps falter, especially if we know that what lies ahead spells trouble. It is here that character is tested. And many of us fail. We call it facing the music. Usually, we don't.

Joy and I got a good close look at this kind of courage the day our little pickup and an 18-wheeler semi ran into each other in Gaithersburg, Maryland. We were driving in heavy rain on our way to her doctor's appointment. Up ahead a car pulled out from a side street and then, according to the truck driver, slowed suddenly, forcing him to hit the brakes. He immediately began hydroplaning, the long trailer fishtailing into our lane. I swerved for the ditch but couldn't escape. The trailer hit us with tremendous force, slapping us across the ditch onto the bank above it and back into the culvert. The engine escaped damage, but the force broke off a rear wheel, tore the axle loose, separated the drivetrain, and, as if by a huge can opener, sliced a gash in the driver's side from the rearview mirror to the rear bumper. My door wouldn't open and Joy's was against the bank. After making certain she was not seriously hurt, I crawled over her and out her window. It was only then I realized the truck had kept going.

He had hit and run! I couldn't believe it. Fortunately two witnesses quickly arrived so they could offer their services as witnesses, one of them standing with me in the rain until the police arrived after what seemed like a very long time. Because of the rain, ours was not their only accident that day on Gaithersburg's slick streets.

The officer took the testimonies of the witnesses, wrote down all the information she needed from us, and shook her head over the callous driver's flight from the scene. He wouldn't get away with it, she assured us. By putting together all the facts the witnesses gave her (I could barely tell her my name!), she knew the police would find him soon.

They didn't have to look. He returned. After bringing his jackknifing semi under control, he had driven on to his destination and unloaded his cargo. Then, because he thought he might have hit something when he was fighting to steady his careening ship, he drove back down the highway, saw us still in the ditch, moved his rig to the next side street, and reported to the police officer. He was shaken, in part because of the damage he saw he had done to us, but also because he now had to face his employer. There would be a drug test. Someone else would have to drive his truck away, which was company policy.

I commended him for returning. It was not easy for him to face the police officer, his supervisor, or us. There would be consequences. But he faced the music.

Where does the courage "to face the music" come from?

### Courage Comes from Knowing You Have No Other Acceptable Choice

Jesus went to Jerusalem even though He knew what lay in store for Him. He went because He had no choice. No acceptable one, that is. He didn't have to go. He could have remained in friendlier Galilee. He could have tempered His teaching, softened His retorts to His critics, and placated the Pharisees. He could have returned to the carpenter's shop. He could have blended in with the crowd, retreating into the anonymity that shields from trouble.

He could have if He hadn't cared so much about His mission. But because more than anything else He wanted to finish the job His Father had sent Him to do, He had no acceptable alternative. He had to go to Jerusalem.

## Courage Comes from Knowing That
## If You Don't Act, Nobody Else Will

Sometimes you may be the only one who can act. Only Jesus could do for us what He did on the cross. But many times there are others who can act but don't. The cost is too high, the risk too great.

Parents, if we aren't careful, we will teach our children to be afraid instead of bolstering their courage. We rightfully warn Johnny and Suzie against running with the wrong crowd but wrongfully neglect the cautionary word about just *running* with any crowd. There are certain parts of town we tell them not to go into, certain hangouts that are off-limits. We don't want them to get into avoidable trouble. But often it isn't the place that threatens, but the crowd itself. If there is anything we should encourage them to be afraid of, it is of uncritically going along with the crowd. As Soren Kierkegaard insists:

> There is no place, not even one most disgustingly dedicated to lust and vice, where a human being is more easily corrupted—than in the crowd.
>
> Even though every individual possesses the truth, when he gets together in a crowd, untruth will be present at once, for the crowd *is* untruth. It either produces impenitence and irresponsibility or it weakens the individual's sense of responsibility by placing it in a fractional category. For instance, imagine an individual walking up to Christ and spitting on him.[29]

Reread Luke's Gospel. Note how often Jesus was *against* the crowd, sometimes even against His own disciples. Throughout His ministry, He was surrounded by people, some for Him, some against Him. They saw the same opportunities to do good that He did, but they didn't act. He did.

"For God so loved the world that he gave his one and only Son" (John 3:16). He sent an individual. He did not send a committee. He was well aware of the old saw that nothing is impossible until it is sent to a committee. (A committee, it is good to remember, is but a small crowd.)

Paul Tillich, whose title *The Courage to Be* was mentioned earlier, defines *courage* in that book as "strength of mind, capable of conquering whatever threatens the attainment of the highest good."[30] His is a good working definition of this indispensable virtue. Though hostile crowds were waiting for Jesus in Jerusalem, the highest good to which He had pledged himself compelled Him to go forward anyway.

### Courage Comes from Accepting That Any Good You Do Will Upset Somebody

Nothing has been harder to deal with in my ministry than this fact. I have had no trouble accepting criticism when I've been wrong, which has been often enough. What has been almost unbearable at times has been the predictable, irrational, sometimes vicious condemnation I have received when I've been right! No wonder we delegate difficult decisions to a committee. We aren't so much afraid of being wrong as we are of being alone. That's why the standard teenage argument is, "But everybody's doing it!" The fear of being an oddball can make cowards of us all. In our minds we aspire to nobility. We want to do right, to be decent, to live honorably. But the cost! "Socrates was forced to drink hemlock for his pains. Jesus was crucified. Abraham Lincoln and Martin Luther King, Jr. were assassinated, and Joe Bloggs loses his job for blowing the whistle. How can I adapt," Peter J. Gomes asks, "the values and virtues of the good life for my life and world, which are less than perfect?"[31] Unfortunately, we can't. Even Jesus couldn't.

On another Sabbath he went into the synagogue
and was teaching, and a man was there whose
right hand was shriveled. The Pharisees and the
teachers of the law were looking for a reason to
accuse Jesus, so they watched him closely to see
if he would heal on the Sabbath. But Jesus knew
what they were thinking and said to the man with
the shriveled hand, "Get up and stand in front of
everyone." So he got up and stood there.

Then Jesus said to them, "I ask you, which is
lawful on the Sabbath: to do good or to do evil, to
save life or to destroy it?"

He looked around at them all, and then said to
the man, "Stretch out your hand." He did so, and
his hand was completely restored. But they were
furious and began to discuss with one another
what they might do to Jesus (Luke 6:6-11).

The more good Jesus did, the greater the resentment against
Him. Yet He continued "to boldly go . . ."

## Courage Comes from Believing in "The Rest of the Story"

Jesus did not minimize the fate waiting for Him in Jerusalem.
"We are going up to Jerusalem, and everything that is written by
the prophets about the Son of Man will be fulfilled. He will be
handed over to the Gentiles. They will mock him, insult him, spit
on him, flog him and kill him" (Luke 18:31, 32). This time His
enemies would not be out-maneuvered. They would get Him.

He would go to Jerusalem anyway. His future looked grim,
but it didn't end with Jerusalem. There were immediate consequences to be faced; there were also long-term consequences
to be enjoyed. The end of the story makes the rest of the story
bearable: "On the third day he will rise again" (v. 33).

The writer of Hebrews identifies this source of Jesus' courage and challenges us to hang on to that same source:

> Let us fix our eyes on Jesus, the author and perfecter of our faith, who for the joy set before him endured the cross, scorning its shame, and sat down at the right hand of the throne of God. Consider him who endured such opposition from sinful men, so that you will not grow weary and lose heart (Hebrews 12:2, 3).

Since Jesus did it, the writer says, we can. These sentences could serve as the scriptural text for this entire study. Consider Jesus' character—then imitate it. Look to His source of courage, and hang on to it. Then "you will not grow weary and lose heart."

# 8
# Built for Loyalty

## Luke 6:12-16; 22:1-6

{
And Judas went to the chief priests and the
officers of the temple guard and discussed
with them how he might betray Jesus
(Luke 22:4).
}

Indira Gandhi's assassination in November 1984 shocked
the world. In her second term as prime minister of India, Mrs.
Gandhi was successfully guiding her religion-wracked nation
through yet another crisis. She had earned the respect, if not
always the approval, of world leaders for her mastery of her
country's complex political realities. She was an admired but
also fervently hated woman.

Like other public personalities, Mrs. Gandhi went nowhere
without the protection of her guard. Fearsome Sikhs made up
the contingent that never left her side. One of them, Beant Singh,
was a favorite. She had known him for 10 years. When she was
asked whether she could trust her Sikh guards, he was the one
she pointed out. With him at her side, she had nothing to fear.

The question was raised because of her controversial decision
to send the army to Amritsar in the Punjab—the site of the Sikhs'
holiest shrine known as the Golden Temple—to squelch Sikh

extremist activity there. Mrs. Gandhi instantly became *persona non grata* to the radicals. Moderates feared for her safety. Not to worry, she assured them; she had Beant Singh to protect her.

But he killed her. He and a fellow Sikh, Satwant Singh, had been assigned to Mrs. Gandhi's detail five months before. They waited for their opportunity, then struck. Standing no more than seven feet away as she greeted them, Beant Singh shot his .38 revolver three times into her abdomen. As she fell, Satwant Singh pumped all 30 rounds from his Sten automatic weapon into her crumpled body.[32] Where do you turn when your guards attack? Who protects you from your protectors?

Loyalty is among the very highest of virtues, disloyalty the most contemptible of character flaws. In *The Divine Comedy*, Dante consigned Judas, the traitor, to the bottom of Hell. He deserved the worst. Of course Judas was a much smoother operator than Beant Singh and Satwant Singh. No blood, no violence. Just a kiss. The kiss of death.

> While he was still speaking a crowd came up, and the man who was called Judas, one of the Twelve, was leading them. He approached Jesus to kiss him, but Jesus asked him, "Judas, are you betraying the Son of Man *with a kiss?*"
> (Luke 22:47, 48, italics mine).

This, as Shakespeare's Mark Antony would say of Julius Caesar's assassin, was "the most unkindest cut of all."

## Judas's Betrayal—the Polar Opposite of Loyalty

As you have already gathered, this chapter is a departure from the other nine because in the Gospel accounts, this character trait may best be studied through its polar opposite—disloyalty. Here we will look closely at one of Jesus' disciples; in the other chapters, we are studying Jesus himself. We want to become more like Him. One of His most admirable qualities, His loyalty to His Father and His followers, permeates everything He does. You simply cannot imagine Jesus being disloyal. It's unthinkable.

But Judas is another story. In him we have a talented man who goes bad, so bad that his name is now a synonym for disloyalty. When Luke introduces the disciples to his readers, he merely names most of them—"James, John, Philip, Bartholomew, Matthew, Thomas"—and briefly shows the relationships among some others—"his [Peter's] brother Andrew, . . . James son of Alphaeus, Simon who was called the Zealot, Judas son of James." He describes only two of them: "Simon (whom he [Jesus] named Peter)," and "Judas Iscariot, who became a traitor." (See Luke 6:13-16.) The outstanding characteristic of Judas, as far as Luke was concerned, was his disloyalty. He is the model of what a disciple of Jesus does not want to become.

For 2,000 years, Bible students have been trying to understand or explain or even justify Judas. Why did he do it? What was his motive? Was it his zeal to overturn the Roman occupiers of Israel? Was it personal ambition? Was it his bitter disappointment with Jesus? Some writers blame Jesus because He surely must have known Judas's heart. Did Jesus set him up? Was Judas manipulated to sell Jesus out in order to trigger events that led to the planned crucifixion?

The speculation leads nowhere. As far as Luke was concerned, the explanation is simple:

{ Now the Feast of Unleavened Bread, called the Passover, was approaching, and the chief priests and the teachers of the law were looking for some way to get rid of Jesus, for they were afraid of the people. *Then Satan entered Judas,* called Iscariot, one of the Twelve. And Judas went to the chief priests and the officers of the temple guard and discussed with them *how he might betray Jesus.* They were delighted and *agreed to give him money. He consented,* and *watched for an opportunity to hand Jesus over to them when no crowd was present* (Luke 22:1-6, italics mine).

Look again at each italicized section:

- *Then Satan entered Judas*—By this point, Judas has lost his self-control. He has renounced his allegiance to Jesus. He has a new master. As we would put it today, "He's gone to the devil."

- *How he might betray Jesus*—Judas's kiss is not impulsive. Emotion hasn't overwhelmed him. It is deliberate, premeditated treachery.

- *Agreed to give him money*—Did he ask? Did he bargain with his backers? "If you'll pay me so much, I'll do such and such. . . ." If he did, the act seems even more despicable than ever. He betrayed his friend *for money?* Not for a principle, for patriotism, or some other worthy, defensible reason?

- *He consented*—To what? Was the money their idea? Were there stipulations Judas had to agree to?

- *Watched for an opportunity to hand Jesus over when no crowd was present*—So he became, at last, a cowardly sneak.

It's a terrible picture that Luke gives us. But can you think of anything much worse than to be betrayed by your trusted friend?

# A Test of Character

What makes loyalty such a tough test of character is its demand that we act in opposition to our natural selfishness. Whatever else his motive might have been, Judas was taking care of Judas. He was "looking out for Number One," which, unfortunately, is the basic ethic of our society. If Jesus is the model of the person we want to be, we turn away from Judas because we recognize in him the person that we, for the most part, are!

Consider an organization, any organization, in which all persons look out primarily for their own interests. What happens in the family, the most basic of organizations, when the members disregard the needs of others and care only about their own desires? Is there any way to hold them together? Waiting in line for a ride at Disney World recently, I stood beside a Georgia schoolteacher who bewailed the plight of that state's schools. He said children were taught not to pledge allegiance to the American flag. On parent-teacher conference day, he lamented, parents sometimes bring their attorneys! He hated his job and feared for the future of the country because the only loyalty the children were being taught was loyalty to their own interests.

I hoped he was exaggerating. I suspect he was. Yet evidence of the "me-first" ethic abounds where you live too, doesn't it?

At the time of Joy's and my visit to Disney World, by the way, I was reading a book on leadership, *Shackleton's Way*. It's a study of the adventures of Sir Ernest Shackleton, the great Antarctica explorer. Several movies have recently been made of this extraordinary man's feats, the greatest of which was his failed attempt to cross the continent of Antarctica on foot. When the ice locked his ship *Endurance* in its unforgiving grip, he had to face the fact that his original goal could not be met.

There was no way he and his men could cross Antarctica. His new challenge, from which he did not flinch, was even more daunting: getting his men home alive.

Sir Ernest was not a novice explorer. He had been part of Robert F. Scott's three-man Farthest South team in 1902 that fell 460 miles short of reaching the South Pole. Six years later he commanded his own expedition; that time he was forced to turn around just 97 miles short of his goal to keep his team from starvation. That was still such a remarkable feat that he was knighted for it. His 1914–1916 *Endurance* expedition was "his greatest failure." In his case, the word is a compliment. He lost his ship (trapped and then crushed by ice) before ever touching Antarctica. He and his men were stranded on an ice floe more than 1,200 miles from the farthest outpost of civilization. They were left with three rickety lifeboats and a few provisions.

The testimony of his men was that, against all odds, they were kept alive by their belief in and loyalty to "the Boss," as they affectionately termed Shackleton. He, on the other hand, said that his responsibility for them was what kept him going. Loyalty goes both directions.

Shackleton believed that the loyalty of his men was a sacred trust, one never to be betrayed. He once spelled out for a friend his view of life:

> The chief end is to win it [the game of life] honorably and splendidly. To this chief end several things are necessary. Loyalty is one. Discipline is another. Unselfishness is another. Courage is another. Optimism is another. And Chivalry is another.[33]

That he places loyalty at the head of his list is not surprising in view of his life's work. In attempting to save his men's lives, if there were risks to be taken, he took them. If there were sacrifices to be made, he made them. If anyone had to go without food so others could eat, he denied himself. Not for glory, but because of loyalty. They trusted him; he must not betray that trust.

As a result, nearly 100 years after "his greatest failure," Shackleton's reputation is at its peak and his fame continues to be spread. Judas is his polar opposite.

There are four dimensions of loyalty that bear a closer look.

## Loyal to Your Best Self

It can be argued that we all look out for ourselves, that it's impossible not to. Let's grant that argument. What we can control, though, is which self we look out for. As disciples of Jesus, we want to serve our best selves.

For Dag Hammarskjöld, that still means looking out for others. "Don't be afraid of yourself, live your individuality to the full—but for the good of others."[34] I've been quoting this man for years. He was secretary general of the United Nations at the time of his death in a plane crash in the mid-1960s. His published "markings" were originally private notes to himself. They formed the basis of his self-improvement program. It's instructive that this powerful, brooding, introverted yet very public man found that he could be loyal to his best self only through living for the good of others.

There was nothing peculiarly Christian in Hammarskjöld's discovery. You'll find a similar expectation in many cultures. Much of the Christian ethic derives from ancient Israel, so we turn to the Old as well as the New Testament for guidance. Nowhere in these Scriptures do we find that loyalty to your best self stands in opposition to your loyalty to others.

The same is true in ancient Greek and Roman civilizations, the other primary source of Western civilization. In Rome, public, not private, life was extolled. Architecture, theater, poetry, and oratory were for public appreciation and edification. One's "private" life was lived in public. Our term *idiot* comes from the Latin (Rome's language) *idiota* (and the Romans got the word from the Greek *idiots*), which means "private person." We get our word *idiosyncrasy* from the same root. Even today, then, a purely private person is an "idiot," undoubtedly displaying several "idiosyncrasies"! It is, if you please, "idiotic" to seek your personal pleasure only, without regard to others—the public. Jesus' words ring true: "For whoever wants to save his life will lose it, but whoever loses his life for me will find it" (Matthew 16:25). He will find, that is to say, his best self.

## Loyal to Another (Friend, Boss, Loved One)

Over the Christmas holiday our grandchildren were given the video of Disney's *Pirates of the Caribbean*. If you have seen it, you know it's a most unlikely tale of "the worst pirate I've ever seen." It's an amusing, nonsensical romp. Several crises are averted (or at least altered) when a character invokes "the Code," the rigid set of behavioral standards that define a pirate's ethic. Even swashbuckling villains are called to account. Topping the Code's commandments is the expectation that pirates who have sworn allegiance to their captain will be loyal to him and to each other.

The grandkids also received a tape of another Disney production, *Finding Nemo*. This tale of a clownfish father's desperate search for his little son in the depths of a hostile sea, and the son's adventures while trapped in a dentist's fish tank, is another morality play exploring the costs and consequences of loyalty. In fact, can you think of a really good movie or novel that does not touch on this theme?

One reason for much unhappiness is people's failure to learn the lesson—or to submit to the demands—of loyalty. Have you noticed a similar thread running through many recent commercials? Playing on the human resistance to restraint, they trumpet the call of freedom. An Isuzu Rodeo commercial claims, "The world has boundaries. Ignore them." It announces this as an Isuzu topples a huge sign that says "Rules." Then there's Burger King's "Sometimes, you gotta break the rules," and Outback Steakhouse's "No rules. Just right" and Neiman Marcus's "No rules here," and the Columbia House Music Club's "We broke the rules" and Comedy Central's "See comedy that breaks rules."[35]

This appeal to human rebelliousness may sell goods, but its end is the collapse of relationships. If there's no "code" of conduct, if I can do anything I want whenever I want, if "you gotta break the rules" in order to get ahead, if I don't have to be loyal to you or anybody else, then living together in community is impossible.

The climate of the times is graphically exhibited in a cartoon depicting a husband and wife sitting in their comfortable living room chairs, each reading a book. His is entitled, *The Art of Submitting to Your Husband.* Hers, *How to Really Love Your Wife.* If I owe you nothing, then it is really all about me and how you should treat me.[36] You don't matter.

## Loyal to a Cause

Excuse Judas if you will, but you can't get around the fact that, no matter how noble his motivation might have been, he still betrayed his friend. And in betraying Jesus, he betrayed the mission for which he signed on.

According to John's Gospel, Judas may never have been loyal. John calls him a thief, because "as keeper of the money bag, he used to help himself to what was put into it" (12:6). He stole from the company funds. Since it was all about him, he could convince himself that "what's theirs is mine." He reminds us of the infamous Ivan Boesky, who believes, you'll remember from Chapter 6, that "greed is all right . . . greed is healthy. You can be greedy and still feel good about yourself."[37] Of course you can. That's what looking out for Number One is all about. You feel you can break all the rules because they don't apply to you. You are loyal to no one or nothing else but yourself because you are the only cause that matters.

Boesky's creed (with its consequences) is precisely what Jesus addresses in Luke 16:10-15:

> Whoever can be trusted with very little can also be trusted with much, and whoever is dishonest with very little will also be dishonest with much. So if you have not been trustworthy in handling worldly wealth, who will trust you with true riches? And if you have not been trustworthy with someone else's property, who will give you property of your own? (Luke 16:10-12).

Judas proved untrustworthy with the little bag of the disciples' money. Should it surprise anyone that he was disloyal to the disciples' leader? He took their coins (a little thing); he did not scruple to take their leader's life (a very big thing).

> No servant can serve two masters. Either he will hate the one and love the other, or he will be devoted to the one and despise the other. You cannot serve both God and Money (Luke 16:13).

Jesus' audience couldn't accept this. They, like people everywhere ever since, loved money too much to see what it was doing to their relationships with God and everybody else. They would not admit that once you've pledged your allegiance to money, you have no more allegiance to pledge.

> The Pharisees, who loved money, heard all this
> and were sneering at Jesus. He said to them, "You
> are the ones who justify yourselves in the eyes of
> men, but God knows your hearts. What is highly
> valued among men is detestable in God's sight"
> (Luke 16:14, 15).

It is detestable because in their heart there was no room for Him. They had made their choice and He wasn't chosen.

## Loyal to Your God

This is the lament of the prophets. Jeremiah's complaint could be that of the contemporary American preacher calling his people back to the God they've forgotten:

> This is what the LORD says:
> "What fault did your fathers find in me,
>   that they strayed so far from me?
> They followed worthless idols
>   and became worthless themselves.
> They did not ask, 'Where is the LORD,
>   who brought us up out of Egypt
>   and led us through the barren wilderness,
>   through a land of deserts and rifts,
>   a land of drought and darkness,
>   a land where no one travels and no one lives?'
> I brought you into a fertile land
>   to eat its fruit and rich produce" (Jeremiah 2:5-7).

Once again ingratitude is to blame (see Chapter 6). Without a thankful heart, friendship cannot be sustained. Without a thankful heart, loyalty is but an empty word. Jeremiah regrets the disloyalty of the whole nation of Israel. The people have forgotten how much God has done for them. Where ingratitude abounds, infidelity reigns. So they turned to other gods and made up their own rules.

> The Lord says:
> "These people come near to me with their mouth
>     and honor me with their lips,
>     but their hearts are far from me.
> Their worship of me
>     is made up only of rules taught by men"
> (Isaiah 29:13).

Jesus says it even more strongly: "You nullify the word of God for the sake of your tradition. You hypocrites!" (Matthew 15:6, 7).

When something happens that calls people back to God, the world marvels at the difference in them. Shortly after the September 11 terrorist attacks, Max Lucado wrote to his friend Bruce Wilkinson, "This is a different country than it was a week ago. We're not as self-centered as we were. We're not as self-reliant as we were. Hands are out. Knees are bent. This is not normal. And I have to ask the question, 'Do we want to go back to normal?' Perhaps the best response to this tragedy is to refuse to go back to normal."[38] With terrorists threatening, Americans turned to God and loved one another.

More than two years later, it's once again business as usual. Church attendance has dropped back to its preattack levels. Partisan carping is as loud as ever. The economy has been rebounding. The consumer is doling out the cash in record spending. And God has been shown to His usual backseat.

Yet there is a difference, I believe. We got a glimpse of our best selves after the Twin Towers collapsed. We saw our national leaders hold hands and sing, and television cameras followed them into churches and cathedrals where they prayed. For a while, political differences were shelved while the nation repaired the damage. We acted, for a while, like people who loved God and loved each other.

We sampled the fruit of loyalty. "In God we trust" was more than a motto stamped on our money. We trusted. And our national return to God brought out the best in us.

It didn't last, but it hasn't disappeared completely either. We will remember that immediately after September 11, in the words of the songs we sang with new fervor, America *is* beautiful. God *has blessed* America.

Remembering, we will be loyal to God, to our best selves, to others, and to the cause to which we have pledged our lives.

# 9
# Built for Integrity
### Luke 13:10-17

> The Lord answered him, "You hypocrites!
> Doesn't each of you on the Sabbath untie
> his ox or donkey from the stall and
> lead it out to give it water? Then should
> not this woman . . . be set free on the
> Sabbath day from what bound her?"
> (Luke 13:15, 16).

Will you allow me one more Ben Franklin story? Twenty years before the American colonies declared their independence from England, Franklin, as a responsible civic leader, headed a militia (there was no standing army, so defense was in the hands of civilian soldiers). He was 50 years of age, continuing to show the cleverness that had energized his career ever since he left home as a teenager. He enjoyed his military stint, as he seemed to enjoy just about everything else he did. Among his other accomplishments, Franklin was able to get the 500 soldiers under his command to attend worship services. He assigned the chaplain the task of doling out the men's daily allotment of rum—following the service. "Never were prayers more generally and punctually attended."[39] No doubt.

Franklin's ploy reminds me of the several times I was the guest speaker at a downtown mission or some other quasi-religious event when first came the sermon, then the food. It was pretty easy to tell that religion was not top priority for the participants. They had come to eat! They were not, as you can well imagine, the most receptive audience.

## Hypocrisy—What You See Is *Not* What You Get

Which leads to a question that must haunt every pastor or other religious leader: Why *did* they come? Are they here to worship the Lord or for some other, more self-serving reason? Did they come for the doctrine or the donuts?

The real issue is not with them though, is it? It's more personal. Why did *I* come? What do *I* expect to get out of it? And for religious leaders, the question can be even more painful. Why am I doing this? What is my motive? Do I really believe what I am saying?

Many are the wives who've dragged their husbands to church, hoping it'll do *them* some good. Many are the members who religiously observe the rituals and perform what they understand to be the duties of the faith without ever intending to let their observances change them.

We call such people *hypocrites*, from the Greek word for actor. They are playacting their religion. They exhibit the form of religiousness but their hearts are not in it. What you see is not what you get. We learned this word *hypocrite* from Jesus. It was His apt description of the religious leaders who dogged His trail. They carefully burnished their reputation for piety, but Jesus, who saw into their hearts, was not impressed.

*Hypocrite* was not their word for themselves, of course. They did not consider themselves phony. They scrupulously crossed every religious *t* and dotted every spiritual *i*. They studied the Law of Moses and did their best to live up to it. And as for their hostility toward Jesus, their passion to shut Him up was exactly what they believed their religion demanded. They acted as appointed (or self-appointed) guardians of the faith. In their way of thinking, Jesus was a dangerous heretic, disobeying the Law and encouraging others to do so. They were the spiritual ones; He was the pervert.

In a sense, they were right. From their point of view, He was warping sound doctrine. They knew their Torah. What this man was teaching was something else. To silence Him was their duty. They were prepared to kill in order to protect their community. They were no different from the radicals waging today's religious wars.

When Jesus called them hypocrites, though, He was not judging them by their standards or their understanding of their religion, but by His. Reading the same sacred Scriptures they read, He came to very different conclusions. Their attention was riveted on the hundreds of dos and don'ts that would make them God-pleasers. Jesus, with His deeper insight into God's will, concluded that they might claim to love God but could not say the same for loving their neighbors. They were only half right.

At the very end of Jesus' ministry, for example, Luke writes that "the teachers of the law and the chief priests looked for a way to arrest him immediately, *because they knew he had spoken this parable against them*" (Luke 20:19, italics mine). They would charge Him with teaching against God; their real concern was that He was teaching against them. Hypocrisy.

"But they were afraid of the people" (v. 19). They maintained their only concern was to obey God, but they would not risk defending God if doing so placed them in harm's way with the people. Hypocrisy.

"Keeping a close watch on him, they sent spies, who pretended to be honest" (v. 20). They would stoop to perjury if that's what it took to bring Jesus down. Truth could be sacrificed. Anything to get Him. Hypocrisy.

They didn't catch Jesus by surprise. Much earlier He had warned His followers to "be on your guard against the yeast of the Pharisees, which is hypocrisy." He assured them that "there is nothing concealed that will not be disclosed, or hidden that will not be made known. What you have said in the dark will be heard in the daylight, and what you have whispered in the ear in the inner rooms will be proclaimed from the roofs" (Luke 12:1-3). Here He zeroes in on what makes hypocrisy so noxious. It ferments and expands like yeast until it takes over. It works its way through persons and groups. Masks of respectability cover deceitful faces; truth is whispered, public lies go on display as truth. What you see is not what you get; what you hear won't bear investigation.

## The Real Issue Behind Hypocrisy

The contrast between Jesus' sensitivity to human suffering and the religious leaders' callous disregard is nowhere more clearly seen than in Luke 13:10-17. He is teaching in a synagogue when a woman catches His attention. Luke says that for 18 years she has been so badly afflicted she can no longer straighten up. Jesus can't stand to see her suffer, so He heals her. Her stiff body immediately unbends. She praises God for her deliverance.

The synagogue ruler does not rejoice. A rule has been violated. Perhaps not daring to confront Jesus directly, he lashes out at the people. "There are six days for work. So come and be healed on those days, not on the Sabbath" (Luke 13:14).

However, if they were to come on one of the other six days, there would be no healing because no one else could do the job. That point is irrelevant to the ruler. He has no concern for the woman's health; he's upset that Jesus has violated some rule.

So Jesus lashes back—at the ruler and through him at all who prefer rule keeping to people healing. The ruler himself, Jesus charges, would not scruple on the Sabbath to "untie his ox or donkey from the stall and lead it out to give it water" (Luke 13:15). He wants to know which is more important—caring for the donkey or healing this woman? The letter of the law or the spirit? The compassion of God or the death-grip of Satan? "Then should not this woman, a daughter of Abraham, whom Satan has kept bound for eighteen long years, be set free on the Sabbath day from what bound her?" Jesus asks (Luke 13:16). He doesn't make any friends among His critics that day: "All his opponents were humiliated" (Luke 13:17).

That's the real issue, isn't it? It isn't really about the woman, or even about Jesus, but about pride. He would not have humiliated them if they cared about the woman. They would have been thrilled by the miracle. But to them the more important consequence was that their positions had been compromised and their authority discredited. Jesus had out-healed and out-taught them and, as a result, He'd turned the people's allegiance from them to himself.

Throughout Luke's account, the religious leaders who pit themselves against Jesus do not come out the winners. Adorning their selfish ambitions in costumes of piety, they come across (and are so labeled) as mean playactors whose religion is only rule- and ritual-deep. They are hypocrites.

Let's turn for relief to Luke 19, where a confrontation of another type takes place with far happier results. Here Jesus deals not with a "religious" man but with the very incarnation of worldliness: a successful tax collector. What Sunday school children remember best about Zacchaeus is that he was "a wee little man" who climbed into a tree so he could see Jesus as He passed by. We also know that when Jesus reached the spot where Zacchaeus was perched, He told him to climb down and go home, because Jesus was inviting himself in.

The Sunday school song ended there. The rest of the story wasn't turned into song, the part about Jesus breaking social norms and the people around Him muttering their disapproval. "He has gone to be the guest of a 'sinner'" (Luke 19:7). No self-respecting religious leader would do this, they were sure. But Jesus, who never claimed to be a religious leader, would and did.

Luke doesn't tell us anything about the conversation in Zacchaeus's house. What he does report is the outcome. The wealthy publican, who made his money overcharging his tax-payers, was converted. His conversion had nothing to do with the rules and rituals of religion though. He had probably been observing them all along, even as he extorted money from his victims. No, he was changed at the very core of a tax collector's being—in his pocketbook. A new integrity was transforming his professional life: "Zacchaeus stood up and said to the Lord, 'Look, Lord! Here and now I give half of my possessions to the poor, and if I have cheated anybody out of anything, I will pay back four times the amount'" (Luke 19:8).

A friend showed me a cartoon published after yet another scandal in high places. The defendant, apparently a middle-management type, stands before the judge, who tells him, "To be perfectly honest, I suppose crime sometimes does pay—but not at your level."[40] At Zacchaeus's level, it had been paying well for many years. His "crime" didn't land him before a judge's bench; what he did was not illegal. He had contracted with Rome to raise a certain amount of tax revenue for the empire. Anything he could gain for himself beyond what he owed Rome was his to keep. A tax collector was expected to operate in the gray area between complete honesty and looking out for his own interests.

But something happened to Zacchaeus when he was with Jesus. Gray was no longer good enough. He would not steal, he would not cheat, and he would no longer take unfair advantage of people. He had discovered integrity.

When Franklin Pierce was inaugurated as fourteenth president of the United States, he did something unique among all our presidents. He "affirmed" rather than "swore" his loyalty to the Constitution. Taking literally Jesus' teaching not to swear but to let your "yes" be "yes" and your "no" be "no," he exercised the constitutional provision allowing him to say, "I do solemnly affirm," rather than, "I solemnly swear." (See Matthew 5:33-37.)

Pierce's break with tradition was the new president's attempt to ease some of the guilt he felt over his son's death. Less than two months before the inauguration, 11-year-old Benjamin was killed in a train accident. This was the Pierces' third child to die, the other two through illness. The parents were devastated. The president believed Benjamin's death may have been God's punishment for his own sins and for his never having openly professed his faith. By affirming rather than swearing, and by citing the Scripture enjoining against swearing, he was also publicly affirming his faith. He was saying, no more hiding, no more hypocrisy.[41]

## The Church's Problem with Integrity

Above I mentioned that the leaven of the Pharisees—hypocrisy—infects both individuals and groups. The group that the readers of this study care most about is the church, which regrettably is not guiltless. Because of its high standards and its widely diverse congregations, the church invites—and sometimes deserves—criticism for not living up to those standards. Among the most extreme judgments I have read is the following one in, of all places, a Christian magazine. Written by the anonymous columnist Eutychus, the supposedly satirical article stings too smartly to be humorous. In place of such ads as "The Friendly Church" or "A Place to Grow," he proposes "truth in advertising":

- "We can't stand sin, and we like sinners even less."

- "Our church is about as lively as a 91-year-old (in dog years) basset hound."

- "If you show up at our door, you'd better be in a three-piece suit. And if you think someone will say 'Hi' to you, forget it."

- "Come as you are, but be sure to leave your mind at the door."

- "We've had some financial problems lately, and we want your money."

- "You'll feel right at home here—if you don't wear a beard, a pantsuit, necklaces, bracelets, or earrings, and have never heard of Sandi Patti." [42]

Some congregations deserve the rebuke. Far more, in my opinion, do not. Most, though, struggle to live up to their high calling. This has been true from the beginning. Hence the scriptural admonition to "live a life worthy of the calling you have received. Be completely humble and gentle; be patient, bearing with one another in love. Make every effort to keep the unity of the Spirit through the bond of peace" (Ephesians 4:1-3).

A tough requirement, indeed, for reformed human beings trying to leave their selfish pasts and live on a higher plane. If churches seem to be announcing themselves to be something they aren't, it's understandable. Understandable, but not tolerable.

Historically, the church's record of humility, gentleness, and patience has been pretty disappointing. Enemies of Christianity delight in pointing to the bloody Crusades as examples of the hypocrisy of the followers of the Prince of Peace, or citing the cruelty of the West's traffic in African slavery. Because of these and too many other blights on the church's record, I can't laugh at the following. It's a warning in the monastery library of San Pedro in Barcelona. At first I thought it was meant as a joke, some monk's warped sense of humor, but it may be serious:

> From him that steals, or borrows and returns not, a book from its owner, let it change into a serpent in his hand and rend him. Let him be struck with palsy, and all his members blasted. Let him languish in pain crying aloud for mercy, and let there be no surcease to his agony till he sing in dissolution. Let bookworms gnaw at his entrails in token of the worm that dieth not. And, when at last he goes to his final punishment, let the flames of Hell consume him forever.[43]

Such fuss over a book! As much as I love them and get upset when someone filches one of mine, I have yet to resort to such cursing. It's not possible to square these fiery threats with the scriptural injunction for being "completely humble and gentle; be patient, bearing with one another in love" (Ephesians 4:2). How can Christians ever bring about peace on earth otherwise?

When the orphans and widows are neglected, when church members serve money rather than God, when sexual standards are flouted and their marriages crumble into divorce at the same rate as nonmembers, when Christians cannot be trusted in business dealings, when their word is not their bond and lying is their habit, when numbers do in fact matter more than people, the church is playacting.

John Fletcher lays the responsibility for the church's integrity squarely on the shoulders of the leadership. There was a day, he writes, when a priest or rabbi could count on his office to get him through his responsibilities. "Something ought to be done because 'Father' or 'Rabbi' or 'Pastor' wanted it to be done. The role itself was so much more than the person that it overshadowed individual reality." That time was long ago and far away though. "Such is no longer the case. The personal authenticity of the minister, priest, or rabbi is the greatest strength of any congregation. The inauthenticity of the clergy is the greatest weakness of organized religion."[44]

## The Need for Integrity in Society and the Church

Authenticity. Integrity. Church growth experts say this is the quality today's young adults demand above all else. In their formative years, they've been bombarded with so much advertising they are cynical about all of it. They've been disappointed by so many leaders in business, politics, and religion that they have difficulty believing in any of them. They want their religion to be "for real."

Theirs is not a new concern. Tom Peters and Nancy Austin published their *A Passion for Excellence* (a sequel to Peters's best-selling *In Search of Excellence*) in 1985. In it they refer to "our obsessions with integrity." You'd think they were exhorting Christians to "live a life worthy . . ."

> Thus what is not so obvious throughout this book is that virtually every device we suggest is doomed to be useless unless applied with integrity. Worse than useless, most of these devices, used without integrity, will expose you as a hypocrite of the first order. [ex.: Draw your organization charts "upside

124

{ down" (customers or constituents on top, president or city manager on the bottom) and then provide the same careless service. It won't make an iota of difference. Except that you will become a joke.][45]

Which is what has happened to churches that provide *their* same careless service. You won't do business with a dishonest company; neither will you want to trust an inauthentic church!

Speaking of doing business. . . . Not long ago I, received a letter from a financial institution that I don't know anything about. I do know that I'll never do business with the people there. They aren't honest.

Enclosed with the computer-generated letter was a facsimile check for $50,000. That catches your eye! Then the greeting: "Dear Everett L. Lawson." This also caught my eye, since I almost never use my first name. The writer was not a close friend.

Then the letter: "We are pleased to inform you that your home at 933 N. Lindsay Road has recently been verified as eligible for a low interest second mortgage in the amount shown above. If you would like this amount increased please contact your loan agent below. . . . This program is offered to a very select group of individuals in your community on a limited basis and is subject to qualification and the borrower's financial condition. . . ."

I am automatically suspicious of the "very select group of individuals" approach. It usually means they've written every-body in the zip code, or at least those whose income places them above the poverty level.

Even that ploy might be forgivable, but what ensures that I'll never do business with them is that they claim to have verified that 933 N. Lindsay has been rated eligible for a second home mortgage. There's no house there. That's the address of Central Christian Church. I was the pastor there, not the homeowner. Write me down as favoring honesty!

My figures are out-of-date now, but I suspect the percentages have remained about the same. In 1999, Gallup surveyors questioned 1,013 adults in an honesty poll. Which professions, they asked, were most honest and ethical? The results were, as usual, disheartening. Nurses were at the top, receiving a 73% approval rating. Then came pharmacists at 69%. It's downhill from there: veterinarians, 63%; doctors, 58%; K–12 teachers, 57%; clergy, 56%; judges, 53%; police officers, 52%; dentists, 52%; college teachers, 52%.[46] My two categories (clergy and college teachers) barely passed the halfway mark.

Society is obviously crying for leaders of integrity. Certainly the church is. It wants people who practice what they preach, who are at least what they seem to be (if not more), whose word is their bond. People who aren't on the take. Public servants who serve.

At the final session of a national Christian convention in 2003, the presider closed the meeting with an intended compliment to the speaker, but he didn't hear what he said. The rest of us did. "Greg has been using God to touch our hearts tonight." He meant to give God the credit for using Greg.

In many instances what he actually said might have been closer to the truth. I know the speaker in this case, so I don't believe he was merely using God to manipulate the feelings of his audience, but I have been in many church or churchlike gatherings when the speaker did exactly that. Employing God as the means and not the end, speakers and worship leaders have worked up the audience to a fever pitch, basking in the people's applause for their performances. Charismatic leadership was on display maybe, but integrity wasn't.

Do we expect integrity in the courtroom? It was refreshing to learn that Mahatma Gandhi, in his law practice in South Africa, insisted his clients tell him the whole truth if they wanted him to represent them. If they didn't, he dropped their cases. Gandhi contended that it was a lawyer's duty not to prove the guilty innocent (which seems to be the prevailing practice now) but to "help the court arrive at the truth."[47]

More examples could be given of dishonesty in high places from business, politics, the media, sports, and entertainment. That such instances are so plentiful is just too discouraging. There is no end to these negative illustrations.

Thank God, however, you and I know men and women with integrity. They love the truth for its own sake. They refuse to lie, even when it would appear to their advantage to do so. They don't cheat on their income taxes because they don't cheat, period. For them, honesty is not just the best policy, to be employed for the good it can do them. Honesty, commitment to the truth, is best, period.

We respect such people. They have character.

# 10
# Built to Weather the Toughest Storms
### Luke 6:46-49

{
He is like a man building a house, who
dug down deep and laid the foundation
on rock. When a flood came, the torrent
struck that house but could not shake
it, because it was well built
(Luke 6:48).
}

I'm writing this chapter in the dark. We have no electricity. This morning's weather forecast predicted heavy rains by afternoon, along with high winds and even the possibility of a tornado. The rains started only a little over an hour ago, the winds haven't really kicked up yet, but something—perhaps an auto accident that took out a power line—has caused this power outage. The computer has a little battery energy left before it will black out. I'm not looking forward to the rest of the evening.

It was on a day like this one that Joy and I were in the accident that wiped out our pickup truck. She's out in the storm now. She drove to a meeting in a nearby town, saying she would return by 2:00 P.M. She didn't, but she thoughtfully telephoned at exactly that hour to tell me she would be ready to head for home after completing an errand and not to worry. But it's stormy, we just survived one accident on wet streets, and she's out there alone. It's dark in here and becoming dark out there.

Joy's a good driver. She will be cautious, observant. Still, things happen, even to the best of drivers.

So here I sit, listening to the pounding rain, anxious for her to return, and meditating on Luke's Gospel and the character of Christ. My assignment today is 6:46-49, Luke's version of Jesus' famous parable about what happens to a couple of men in a storm. According to Luke, Jesus told the parable to discourage lip service. If His followers were unwilling to apply His teachings—to do what He told them—they could leave Him.

> Why do you call me, "Lord, Lord," and do not do what I say? I will show you what he is like who comes to me and hears my words and puts them into practice. He is like a man building a house, who dug down deep and laid the foundation on rock. When a flood came, the torrent struck that house but could not shake it, because it was well built. But the one who hears my words and does not put them into practice is like a man who built a house on the ground without a foundation. The moment the torrent struck that house, it collapsed and its destruction was complete (Luke 6:46-49).

In Matthew's rendition of the story, Jesus says the man built on the sand; in this one, he built without a foundation. The result is the same: the house can't withstand the storm. It collapses under pressure.

The critical emphasis in the passage above is: "and puts them into practice." The preceding chapters of this book have made one thing clear, if nothing else. Jesus wasn't all talk and He didn't want His disciples to be all talk either. He did not insist that His followers absorb His teachings just so they could repeat them to one another. He wasn't satisfied with memorized excerpts from His speeches, or brilliant debates on the implications of His words. He was not flattered when they heaped praises on Him and His head was not turned when they worshiped Him. Words were not enough. He wanted action. He kept warning His disciples that severe storms lay ahead. Only strong character could stand up against them.

The parable is a call for the discipline that separates doers from wannabes. Disciples are to be "doers of the word, and not hearers only" (James 1:22, *KJV*). They have trained themselves to perform well under the most difficult circumstances. They are ready.

Three practical guidelines for building a strong character are embedded in this simple parable. We will take a close look at each of them.

## Dig Down Deep

{ He is like a man building a house, who dug
down deep (Luke 6:48).

"Do not pray for easy lives," wrote the great nineteenth-century preacher Phillips Brooks, "pray to be stronger people. Do not pray for tasks equal to your powers; pray for powers equal to your tasks. Then the doing of your work shall be no miracle, but you shall be the miracle."[48] Strange, isn't it? The goal of modern civilization, at least in the Western world, is to live an easy life. Laborsaving devices abound. Conveniences that would have astounded our grandparents are everywhere. This dedication to comfort prevails in spite of the fact that serious students of modern life are convinced we are pampering ourselves to our own detriment. An easy life is a shallow life. Where the "living is easy," words are cheap and truth is scarce.

In another warning parable, Jesus notes how few are the persons in whom the Word of truth can take root:

> A farmer went out to sow his seed. As he was scattering the seed, some fell along the path; it was trampled on, and the birds of the air ate it up. Some fell on rock, and when it came up, the plants withered because they had no moisture. Other seed fell among thorns, which grew up with it and choked the plants. Still other seed fell on good soil. It came up and yielded a crop, a hundred times more than was sown (Luke 8:5-8).

Lest there should be any misunderstanding of the story's meaning (the disciples wanted further explanation), Jesus spelled it out:

> This is the meaning of the parable: The seed is the word of God. Those along the path are the ones who hear, and then the devil comes and takes away the word from their hearts, so that they may not believe and be saved. Those on the rock are the ones who receive the word with joy when they hear it, but they have no root. They believe for a while, but in the time of testing they fall away. The seed that fell among thorns stands for those who hear, but as they go on their way they are choked by life's worries, riches and pleasures, and they do not mature. But the seed on good soil stands for those with a noble and good heart, who hear the word, retain it, and by persevering produce a crop (Luke 8:11-15).

What Jesus terms rootedness in this story, He calls going down deep in the first one. It's what the great pioneering missionary to Africa, Dr. David Livingstone, exhibited when as a young man he knelt in prayer and resolved, "I will place no value on anything I have or possess unless it is in relationship to the Kingdom of God." Again on his 59th birthday, the no longer young man wrote, "My Jesus, my King, my Life, my All;

I again dedicate my whole self to Thee." Early in life and late, he rooted himself in (he went deep into) God's will for his life. So grounded, he persevered through many fierce storms.

The apostle Paul, whose life was seldom free of conflict and danger, weathered the worst with the confidence that the Lord would see him through. When praying for those he had led to the Lord, he asked God to give them the same source of strength that had empowered him:

> I pray that out of his [the Father's] glorious riches he may strengthen you with power through his Spirit in your inner being, so that Christ may dwell in your hearts through faith. And I pray that you, *being rooted and established in love,* may have power, together with all the saints, to grasp how *wide and long and high and deep is the love of Christ,* and to know this love that surpasses knowledge— that you may be filled to the measure of all the fullness of God (Ephesians 3:16-19, italics mine).

His language echoes Jesus', doesn't it? He wants his readers to have depth.

A healthy reminder to those of us who have spent years in an academic setting is also included here. Our goal has been to attain knowledge. Paul insists there is something higher (and deeper) than the accumulation of data. Nothing is wider or longer or higher or deeper than "the love of Christ"—the love with which God through Christ loves us and the love that we have for Him. This love relationship with Him fills us with God himself, for God is love.

Going down deep, then, has less to do with bookish learning (although such discipline is important) than it does with learning to love with the love of God.

## Lay Your Foundation on Something Solid

Humorist Dave Barry defines life as "anything that dies when you stomp on it." Worrier Charlie Brown, lying in his bed pondering the mysteries of the universe, wonders whether life is a multiple choice or a true-false test. The answer comes as a voice out of the dark to tell him that life is a thousand-word essay.

E. B. White commuted for many years between his New York office and New England home. The renowned author of *Charlotte's Web* summarized his life in four lines:

> Commuter—one who spends his life
> In riding to and from his wife;
> A man who shaves and takes a train
> And then rides back to shave again.[49]

Opinions on the meaning of life could be quoted almost endlessly. You could almost say that to live is to philosophize; the search for the meaning of life drives every thoughtful person. "Life is what happens when you are making other plans," is one of the search's more famous discoveries.

The *Peanuts* comic strip has it right: Life is a thousand-word essay. You can bluff your way through true-false and multiple-choice tests, but you need something solid on which to base an essay, as many a hapless student can testify.

Where do you turn, then, to gain that solid something? In the last chapter, some disparaging comments were made about the state of the church. Now let me be very positive. For all its weaknesses, the church stands like a lighthouse in a storm showing the way to the truth. No other institution can match it for teaching the Bible and demonstrating a substantial way of life. In the church, according to Paul, "the manifold wisdom of God should be made known to the rulers and authorities in the heavenly realms" [and, we would add, the earthly ones] (Ephesians 3:10). It is, indeed, "the pillar and foundation of the truth" (1 Timothy 3:15). So Christians still pray in the words of the psalmist: "guide me in your truth and teach me, for you are God my Savior" (Psalm 25:5) and "Your word is a lamp to my feet and a light for my path" (Psalm 119:105). Here is the something solid to build a life on.

When we first learn in Jesus' parable of the men whose houses meet such different fates in the storm, we imagine disasters like torrential rains and floods, earthquakes, fire, tornadoes, hurricanes, and the like. Then we move to personal crises: severe illness, loss of a loved one, debilitating accident, crippling financial reversal, prolonged unemployment, and so on.

But what if the crisis is something we would ordinarily think is good? Here's an example of what I mean: Robert O'Donnell was destroyed as the consequence of doing something very good. In 1987, the 37-year-old fireman/paramedic in Midland, Texas, pulled 18-month-old Jessica McClure from an abandoned well. The world watched this hero-in-the-making on the Cable News Network. The baby had been trapped for nearly 60 hours when O'Donnell succeeded against the odds and set her free. "It was the greatest moment of Robert's life," his mother exulted, " . . . and it was the worst thing that ever happened to him," she had to add.

O'Donnell became an instant celebrity. It was too much for him. All of a sudden it seemed the whole world was watching, approving, applauding. O'Donnell decided to cash in. Soon he was quarreling with his fellow rescuers over the movie rights to the story. He turned on them. He wanted all the acclaim he could get. As *New York Times* reporter Lisa Belkin put it, he was "a man so changed by fame that he no longer belonged in his world, but not changed enough that he could leave that world behind." The newborn celebrity became incensed that his fame didn't pay him better. He turned to painkillers to ease the severe migraine headaches he began suffering. They got the better of him. In a remarkably short time, he lost his job and his wife sued for divorce. He bounced from one situation to another until one day on a deserted West Texas road, he turned his shotgun on himself to put an end to his misery. Neal Gabler says O'Donnell "had become addicted to fame, and the true cause of death was his withdrawal from it." When it was taken away, he had nothing else to live for.[50]

If you follow the daily news, you could add many stories of people whose success destroyed them. They hadn't built on anything solid.

## Don't Substitute Talking Big for Building Well

To people who talked big—"Why do you call me, 'Lord, Lord,' and do not do what I say?"—Jesus told this story of the man whose house was "well built." This is a common theme in His teaching. Not much later Luke writes that while He was teaching, "Jesus' mother and brothers came to see him, but they were not able to get near him because of the crowd. Someone told him, 'Your mother and brothers are standing outside, wanting to see you.'" Jesus did not go to them immediately. Instead, with words that must have perplexed His family, He redefined family from one of blood relationships to one of obedience: "My mother and brothers are those who hear God's word and put it into practice" (Luke 8:19-21). Relationships—and character—are built on deeds, not words.

Fred Smith illustrates this truth in one of his treasured memories. He was in a donut shop in Grand Saline, Texas, where he spotted a young farm couple sitting at the next table.

"After finishing their donuts, he got up to pay the bill, and I noticed she didn't get up to follow him. But then he came back and stood in front of her. She put her arms around his neck, and he lifted her up." That's when Smith realized she was wearing a full-body brace. She couldn't walk. Her husband lifted her out of her chair, backed out the front door, carried her to the pickup truck, and gently placed her on the seat of the truck while every eye in the shop watched. No one spoke. Then "a waitress remarked, almost reverently, 'He took his vows seriously.'"[51] Deeds, not words.

Historian James Thomas Flexner is convinced that "probably the most important single gathering ever held in the United States," took place on March 15, 1783, when General George Washington had to face down the wrath of his own officers. They hadn't been paid and they were angry. Attempting to calm them down and retain their service, Washington spoke of his own devotion to his country and his soldiers, and his trust that in the end the government would come through for the officers. He begged his men not to destroy what they had worked so hard to achieve.

He couldn't touch them. Congress had neglected their pay for too long for a few words from their leader to have any effect. Their mood was anarchical. They weren't going to take any more. General Washington read their mood. He knew his speech hadn't helped, but he didn't sit down. Instead, he reached for a letter he wanted to read them, a "reassuring" word from a congressman. Perhaps he hoped that where his own words had failed, the congressman's would be persuasive.

Taking the paper from his pocket, Washington hesitated. He stared at the paper but didn't speak. The officers instinctively leaned forward, wondering. Then he did something few had ever seen the proud leader do: he put on a pair of eyeglasses. "Gentlemen," he said, "you will permit me to put on my spectacles, for I have not only grown gray but almost blind in the service of my country." The resistance melted. "Hardened soldiers wept. Washington had saved the United States from tyranny and civil discord." Flexner says that "where Washington's rhetoric was found wanting, his weak eyes proved decisive, and men's hearts were won."[52]

The simple act of putting on his glasses reminded Washington's men of his personal sacrifices in the line of duty. Their would-be mutiny was squelched. His deeds proved stronger than their needs.

## Character Is in the Doing

It has often been pointed out that the New Testament writers use the word *Christian* only three times but *disciple* 269 times. They had caught on to Jesus' priorities. His goal was not to get men and women to change their labels (from Jew or pagan or whatever to Christian) or to have them ingest and regurgitate His words, but to make disciplined persons of them, men and women who would hear His radical message and then, even more radically, do it.

Robin Hartman, a librarian at Hope International University, attentively kept the rest of us on the faculty and staff advised of her latest Internet discoveries. These were usually helpful research tools. On one occasion, though, her sharp eye found a picture she had to share with us, a photograph of a city billboard reading, "Christ died for our . . ." You couldn't see the word *sins* because it was blotted out by another sign in the foreground advertising Dunkin' Donuts®. Christ died for our Dunkin' Donuts®!

I've kept the picture. It's a good symbol of the trivializing of the gospel. If we blow off the crucifixion, we'll give ourselves to nothing more important than donuts. We may wear the label Christian to distinguish ourselves from the great unwashed ("Of course I'm a Christian. My family has been Christian for seven generations"), but discipleship, not a new label, is what Jesus calls us to.

An early inspiration in my life was the disciple Albert Schweitzer, an accomplished word man who became a world-renowned "doer." A brilliant scholar with gifts in several fields, Dr. Schweitzer devoted his young adult years to pastoral ministry, science, and music, earning distinctions in each field. Then he determined that at 30, he would give the rest of his life in the service of mankind. After receiving his doctorate in medicine in 1913, he left for the Ogowe in equatorial Africa. He served there until his death in 1965. He was not content to be a hearer (student) only; he had to do. His name was disciple.

Yesterday I received word that a dear friend had died. For many years, a weak heart curtailed Dr. Woodrow Phillips's activities. After a lifetime of ministry in America, on the foreign mission field, and in education, he had to slow his pace. Slow, but not stop. Trusting his pacemaker to keep him upright, he kept on serving on mission boards, addressing conventions, and helping churches for as long as he was able. Never content to be a hearer only, he *did* the Word of God. He was a disciple.

Woody belongs to a large company of friends who have built well. Reflecting on his life and death has caused me to think of men and women I have worked with in the church. Most are in their retirement years now. Several have been forced to lighten the load, but they still contribute what they are able. They are indestructible. They have built well. Some of them are gone now. One of them I still miss, especially when I am writing books. Margaret Speas was my secretary for 20 years. She retired from Central Christian Church when I concluded my ministry there. She was 86. She had never missed a day of work. In fact, she worked until within a few months of her death.

Several years earlier she had given me a clipping that I think I already used in one of my books, but which I want to use now to conclude this study. Margaret would be embarrassed to have me talk about her this way because she preferred to work quietly in the background. She was a woman of few words who built a solid life. She was a doer, not a talker. She had character. This is the clipping:

> Cancer is so limited.
> It cannot cripple love,
> It cannot shatter hope,
> It cannot corrode faith,
> It cannot eat away peace,
> It cannot destroy confidence,
> It cannot kill friendship,
> It cannot shut out memories,
> It cannot silence courage,
> It cannot invade the soul,
> It cannot reduce eternal life,
> It cannot quench the Spirit,
> It cannot lessen the power of the resurrection.

Margaret died of cancer. The sickness rapidly took her body, but that was all. She weathered the final storm of her life, as she had weathered so many other heartaches and disappointments, with courage and faith. She had built well. She was a woman of character.

Character—it's more than hearing the Word, or talking the Word. It's doing. It is, as Jesus said, being like the man "who comes to me and hears my words and *puts them into practice.*"

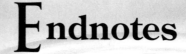

# Endnotes

1. Walter Isaacson, *Benjamin Franklin: An American Life* (New York: Simon & Schuster, 2003), p. 90.
2. Ibid., p. 92.
3. Dan Rather, *The Camera Never Blinks* (New York: Ballantine, 1977), pp. 234–236.
4. Isaacson, p. 153.
5. Os Guinness, *The Call* (Nashville, TN: Word Publishing, 1998), p. 186.
6. Bob Russell, "Duty, Not Just Desire," *The Lookout*, August 21, 1994, p. 13.
7. Thomas Schoenbaum, *Waging Peace and War: Dean Rusk in the Truman, Kennedy and Johnson Years* (New York: Simon & Schuster, 1988), p. 46.
8. Dr. Hacib Aouan shared these insights with his fellow medical practitioners at the 11th Annual David Rabin Memorial Lecture at Vanderbilt University Medical Center in Nashville, Tennessee, in 1991. Published in *American College of Physicians*, February 15, 1992, pp. 335–338.
9. Philip Longfellow Anderson, *The Gospel According to Disney* (LaCanada, CA: Longfellow Publishing, 1999), pp. 247–248.
10. F. W. Bourdillon in Robertson Davies, *The Merry Heart* (New York: Viking Press, 1996), p. 6.
11. Robert Coles, *The Moral Intelligence of Children* (New York: Penguin Group, 1997), p. 195.
12. Robert Caro, *Master of the Senate: The Years of Lyndon Johnson*, Vol. 3 (New York: Knopf, 2002).
13. Quoted in Henri J. M. Nouwen, *The Genesee Diary* (New York: Doubleday, 1976), p. 155.

# Endnotes

[14] Merle Miller, *Plain Speaking: An Oral Biography of Harry S. Truman* (New York: Berkley Publishing, 1974), pp. 431–432.

[15] William Barclay, *The Letters of James and Peter* (Edinburgh, Scotland: St. Andrews Press, 1958), p. 158.

[16] Bruce Catton, *The Army of the Potomac: A Stillness at Appomattox* (Garden City, NY: Doubleday, 1953), pp. 276–277.

[17] Arthur Miller, *Timebends* (New York: Grove Press, 1987), pp. 371–372.

[18] Hans Kung, *Signposts for the Future* (Garden City, NY: Doubleday and Co., 1997), p. 108.

[19] David Colbert, *Eyewitness to Wall Street* (New York: Broadway Books, 2001), p. 217.

[20] Paul F. Boller, Jr., *Congressional Anecdotes* (New York: Oxford University Press, 1991), p. 105.

[21] Guinness, pp. 211–212.

[22] Joshua Halberstam, *Everyday Ethics* (New York: Viking, the Penguin Group, 1993), pp. 16–17.

[23] Edgar A. Guest, *Collected Verse of Edgar A. Guest* (Chicago: The Reilley & Lee Co., 1934), pp. 16–17. Reproduced with Permission of The McGraw-Hill Companies.

[24] James Reston, *Deadline: A Memoir* (New York: Random House, 1991), p. 168.

[25] Martin Marty quoted in David Wolfe, private correspondence, April 14, 2002.

[26] Richard Corliss, "The American as Noble Man," *Time*, June 23, 2003, p. 86.

[27] Tony Horwitz, *Blue Latitudes: Boldly Going Where Captain Cook Has Gone Before* (New York: Henry Holt and Company, 2002), p. 5.

[28] Kenneth C. Davis, *Don't Know Much About the Universe* (New York: HarperCollins Publishers, 2001), p. 261.

[29] Soren Kierkegaard, Charles E. Moore, ed., *Provocations: Spiritual Writings of Kierkegaard* (Farmington, PA: The Plough Publishing House, 1999), p. 23.

[30] Paul Tillich, *The Courage to Be* (New Haven, CT: Yale University Press, 1957), p. 7.

[31] Peter J. Gomes, *The Good Life: Truths That Last in Times of Need* (San Francisco: Harper San Francisco, 2002), p. 69.

[32] *Time*, November 12, 1984, pp. 42–48.

[33] Margot Morrell and Stephanie Capparell, *Shackleton's Way: Leadership Lessons from the Great Antarctic Explorer* (New York: Penguin Books, 2001), p. 209.

[34] Dag Hammarskjöld, *Markings* (New York: Knopf, 1965), p. 53.

[35] John Leo, "The Selling of Rebellion," *U.S. News & World Report*, October 12, 1998, p. 18.

[36] Kathy Collard Miller (compiler) and D. Larry Miller, *God's Vitamin "C" for the Spirit* (Lancaster, PA: Starburst Publishers, 1996), p. 204.

[37] Colbert, p. 217.

[38] Collection by the editors of Beliefnet, *From the Ashes: A Spiritual Response to the Attack on America* (Rodale Press and Beliefnet, Inc., 2001), p. 254.

[39] Isaacson, p. 170.

[40] *Cortland Forum*, February 1997, p. 227.

[41] *Context*, March 15, 1997, p. 1. Originally published in *America*, December 7, 1996.

[42] Eutychus (pseudonym), "Truth, If You Dare, in Advertising," *Christianity Today*, September 16, 1991, p. 7.

[43] *Context*, May 15, 1997, p. 8. Originally published in *The New Yorker*, March 17, 1997.

[44] Edward B. Bratcher, *The Walk-on-Water Syndrome* (Waco, TX: Word Books, 1984), p. 35.

[45] Tom Peters and Nancy Austin, *A Passion for Excellence* (New York: Random House, 1985), p. 34.

[46] The survey information was part of Gallup's Annual Honesty Poll, taken in late 1999. Published by Stamat's Quicktakes, "Insights into Research, Planning, and Integrated Marketing," June 21, 2000, p. 2. Downloaded from the World Wide Web in March 2004.

[47] Louis Fischer, *The Life of Mahatma Gandhi*, quoted in Gerald Kennedy, *A Reader's Notebook* (New York: Harper and Brothers, 1953), p. 309.

[48] *Christianity Today*, May 19, 1997, p. 36.

[49] "Definitions: Commuter," Copyright 1925 by E. B. White from *Poems and Sketches of E. B. White* by E. B. White. Reprinted by permission of HarperCollins Publishers Inc.

[50] Neal Gabler, *Life: The Movie: How Entertainment Conquered Reality* (New York: Vintage Books, 1998), p. 191.

[51] Fred Smith, "Commitment," *Leadership*, Winter 1995, p. 38.

[52] Gary L. Thomas, *The Glorious Pursuit: Embracing the Virtues of Christ* (Colorado Springs, CO: NavPress, 1998), p. 58.